"You're not just holding a book. You're holding the potential to unlock a life you've always envisioned. This is more than inspiration—it's a guide to real transformation. Be ready—this book has the power to shift everything.
—Kayla Leon, award-winning, international best-selling author

"Peggy's step-by-step guidance feels like a personal conversation, encouraging and empowering you to manifest a life of abundance, joy, and fulfillment. It's not just a book—it's a life-changing journey.
—Cynthia Kersey, founder and CEO, Unstoppable Foundation

"This book is more than a read—it's an experience that will transform the way you think about success, manifestation, and the boundless power within you. If you're ready to elevate every aspect of your life, this is the book you've been waiting for.
—Roderick Telfer, empowerment consultant

Praise for *The Moment of Alignment*

"This isn't preaching—it's teaching. Buckle up, because this book will change the way you look at things. Are you ready to transform your life?"
—L.L. Tremblay, author of *Seven Roses* and *Light Over Dark*

"In a world where success can often seem elusive, *The Moment of Alignment* reveals the simple yet profound truth that everything begins with how we think, feel, and act right now. Dr. Peggy McColl masterfully guides readers to step into their own power and align with their dreams in a way that feels both effortless and exhilarating."
—Phillip B. Goldfine, Academy Award, Emmy and Tony Award–winning producer

"Grab this book and follow Dr. Peggy McColl page by page. Everything you need to transform your life is here and is very easy to understand and apply. This is the book I wish I had forty-eight years ago when I started my journey on personal self-development."
—Dr. Mark Wallace, pet doctor and author

"I have an entire shelf dedicated to Peggy McColl's books that have inspired my growth, and *The Moment of Alignment* holds a special place among them. It's a reminder I'll return to often."
—Edelmira Murrieta, entrepreneur and author of *Starter Husband*

"Dive in and let Peggy's wisdom illuminate your path to greatness."
—Arielle Ford, author, *The Love Thief*

"This is not just a book—it's a life-changing experience. I wholeheartedly endorse *The Moment of Alignment* and encourage everyone to embrace its lessons and step into their own moments of creation."
—Wunmi Elebute, founder and editor in chief, *BIWE* magazine; CEO, BIWE Consulting

"Drawing from her own journey of resilience and growth, Peggy offers a masterpiece that will inspire readers to embrace their potential for greatness."
—Jayne Lowell, cofounder, S&J Training Solutions Inc.

"Peggy can show you how to create the life you want, no matter where you are right now! This book shows you exactly how to do that concisely. She leads by example, and you will be forever changed once you dig into these pages."
—Brian Proctor, author of *My Father Knew the Secret*

"With profound wisdom and actionable steps, this book is your pathway to living the life you've always envisioned—one moment of creation at a time."
—Judy O'Beirn, president, Hasmark Services Corp.

"Study this and learn from the best! Dr. Peggy McColl delivers this powerful, concise message for all readers to benefit from."
—Rachel Bazzy, international best-selling author, *Courage*

"Dr. McColl's wisdom is a gift to the world, and her words will leave an indelible mark on your heart and mind. Prepare to be inspired, transformed, and ready to embrace your ultimate moment of creation."
—Dr. Hanan Al Mheiri, award-winning mindset coach and founder of Hanan Empire

"Dr. Peggy McColl's compassionate guidance and powerful insights will not only inspire you but also awaken the dormant creator within, empowering you to manifest your dreams and live a life filled with purpose and joy."
—Steve Lowell, multi–award-winning international speaker, past president, Global Speakers Federation

"Peggy delivers a complete, empowering roadmap to create real magic in your life—one inspired moment at a time. This book is a gift to the world, written specifically with YOU in mind."
—Anders Hansen, illusionist, speaker, mentor

THE MOMENT OF ALIGNMENT

THE PRECISE MOMENT WHERE INTENTION BECOMES REALITY

DR. PEGGY McCOLL

Published 2025 by Gildan Media LLC
aka G&D Media
www.GandDmedia.com

THE MOMENT OF ALIGNMENT. Copyright © 2025 by Dr. Peggy McColl. All rights reserved.

No part of this book may be used, reproduced or transmitted in any manner whatsoever, by any means (electronic, photocopying, recording, or otherwise), without the prior written permission of the author, except in the case of brief quotations embodied in critical articles and reviews. No liability is assumed with respect to the use of the information contained within. Although every precaution has been taken, the author and publisher assume no liability for errors or omissions. Neither is any liability assumed for damages resulting from the use of the information contained herein.

Front cover design by David Rheinhardt of Pyrographx

Interior design by Meghan Day Healey of Story Horse, LLC

Library of Congress Cataloging-in-Publication Data is available upon request

ISBN: 978-1-7225-0726-8

10   9   8   7   6   5   4   3   2   1

Dedicated to Mick Petersen

Michael Shawn Petersen,
August 17, 1966–November 26, 2024

Mick was my dear friend, my source of endless laughter, and a true beacon of light in this world.

What began as a client-mentor relationship blossomed into a friendship unlike any other. Mick embodied joy, resilience, and a deep passion for growth. Like me, he faced challenges and rose above them with grace and unwavering strength. His heart was open, his spirit kind, and his desire to uplift others knew no bounds.

Mick left an indelible mark on my life, and his legacy of love and contribution will ripple out far beyond what either of us could imagine. He was one in a billion, and I am forever grateful for the time we shared.

May this book carry forward the essence of our shared belief—that through love, joy, and unwavering faith, we create miracles.

Peggy McColl

Contents

Message from the Author   13

Introduction   15

Part I
Awakening to Your Creative Potential   19

1 The Magical Power Within   21

2 The Tug-of-War: Why Alignment Feels Hard   27

3 The Power within the Moment   35

4 The Hidden Power of Appreciation   41

5 Manifesting Love:
Embracing the Moment with Faith and Feeling   45

6 Denying the Evidence of the Senses   49

7 Transforming Emotional Habits for Success   55

8 The Immediate Manifestation   63

- 9 Rising above Challenges 69
- 10 The Universe Always Has Your Back 75
- 11 Manifesting with Positive Prayer 83
- 12 The Ripple Effect of Choice 87

Part II

Unblocking the Path to Creation 91

- 13 The Truth That Sets You Free 93
- 14 Understanding the Three Levels of Resistance 97
- 15 Recognizing the Blocks on Your Path 103
- 16 The Twelve Blocks Standing between You and Success 105

Part III

Action into Creation: The Tools for Transformation 127

- 17 The Second Wind 129
- 18 Accomplishment through Accountability 135
- 19 A Fresh New Start 139

- 20 The Bridge between Knowing and Becoming 143
- 21 The Power of Pivotal Moments 149
- 22 Bringing the Future into the Present 153
- 23 Anchoring Success: The Power of Intentional Triggers 159
- 24 One Size Does Not Fit All 167
- 25 Alignment Self-Assessment Quiz 171
- 26 The Alignment Blueprint 175
- 27 Creating with Ease and Flow 183
- 28 The Ultimate Moment of Creation: Living as if It Is Already Done 187

Epilogue Your Creation Is Already Done 189

Bonus Chapter Tools for Daily Success and Alignment 191

Bonus Chapter Your Daily Decree for Embracing the Moment of Creation 199

Addendum Anchored in the Words of Creation 203

Acknowledgments 209

About the Author 213

Message from the Author

Dear Reader,

As you hold this book in your hands, I want you to know that the information you're about to read has the potential to change your life—immediately and dramatically. This is not just another book—this is a guide to creating the life you've always dreamed of.

I invite you to read this book as if your life depends on it—because it does. Your dreams, your desires, and your highest potential are all within reach, and this book will help you unlock them. This is the moment when everything can change for you.

The power to manifest the life you want is already within you. What you'll discover here is a simple, profound truth: Your ideal life is waiting for you. It's not somewhere in the future. It's already yours, ready to be realized—right now.

You have everything it takes to create a life of abundance, joy, love, and fulfillment. I am here to guide you through this process, step by step. As you read, feel the shift, feel the excitement, and know that each page is leading you closer to the life you are destined to live. This book is not just for reading—it's for living. It's for creating.

Get ready to transform. The *moment of creation* has arrived.

With love, Peggy

Introduction

I WASN'T SUPPOSED TO make it. Not with the cards I was dealt.

From the outside, my life could have looked like a series of insurmountable obstacles. I grew up in a household shaped by struggle and hardship—a place where scarcity and emotional turbulence were everyday realities. As a teenager, I felt completely lost, overwhelmed by feelings of worthlessness and despair. I believed I was destined to live a life of misery. That belief weighed on me so heavily that I seriously contemplated ending my life.

Even as I moved into adulthood, the challenges kept coming. I faced crippling debt, a painful divorce, and the devastating losses of my brother, father, and mother, all in a short span of time. And in 2021, I was handed a diagnosis of metastatic cancer—a moment that could have easily shattered me.

But here's the truth: long before some of these challenges appeared, I had already begun a journey that would change my life forever. In 1979, I made a decision—a commitment to personal growth and transformation. At first, it was just a glimmer of hope, a tiny seed of possibility in the midst of my pain. But over the decades, that decision grew into a foundation of knowledge, practices, and mindset shifts that allowed me not only to survive life's challenges but to thrive because of them.

Every step of the way, I dove into what I was learning. I applied it relentlessly—sometimes in desperation, sometimes with faith I didn't even know I had—and piece by piece, I began to create a new reality.

Today I am living a life I once thought was impossible. I am happily married to the love of my life, living in a beautiful home, enjoying incredible health, and waking up every day with profound gratitude for the abundance that surrounds me. I've built a multi-million-dollar business, become a *New York Times* best-selling author, and achieved a level of fulfillment that I never dreamed was possible in those dark early years.

I am here in this moment, not just standing but thriving.

Here's the truth: I didn't just stumble upon success, and it wasn't handed to me. I created it. Step by step, moment by moment, I discovered the power within me to transform my reality. If I could do it, so can you.

This book is not about my journey—it's about yours. It's about equipping you with the tools, understanding, and practices to take hold of your life and create a reality that excites you, fulfills you, and brings you profound joy. It's about recognizing the exact moment when intention becomes reality and harnessing that moment to create the life you desire.

The truth I've come to know—which I will share with you—is beautifully simple yet profoundly life-changing: The most powerful moment in our lives is not some distant memory of the past or a dream of the future. It is the moment of now—the *moment of creation*.

For nearly half a century, I have studied the principles of success, transformation, and personal growth. I've uncovered not just a series of ideas but a profound truth: creation is not a one-time

Introduction

event, or something reserved for the universe's grand beginnings. Creation is happening constantly, in every thought we think, every emotion we feel, and every choice we make.

Whether we realize it or not, we are the architects of our reality, shaping our lives with every moment we live.

This book, *The Moment of Alignment,* is your guide to unlocking that power within you. It is not a collection of lofty theories or abstract ideas—it's a practical, actionable blueprint for transforming your life. You will learn the "why" behind the way we are and, more importantly, the "how" to overcome any situation and create the life you've always envisioned.

I will share with you the same principles and techniques that transformed my life. These are the tools I've used to move from despair to abundance, from hopelessness to fulfillment. They are the same tools that I've seen change the lives of countless others.

This book will challenge you to take an honest look at where you are, embrace the power of the present moment, and step boldly into the life you deserve. You'll discover practical skills you can implement immediately—tools that will not only shift your mindset but also create real, tangible results.

As you turn these pages, I encourage you to lean in. Open your heart, open your mind, and allow yourself to imagine the possibilities that await you. This isn't just a book; it's a key. A key to the life you were meant to live. A life filled with purpose, joy, and boundless abundance.

Your transformation begins here, in this moment. Are you ready to step into the most powerful moment of your life? Are you ready to embrace the *moment of creation?*

Let's begin.

Part I
Awakening to Your Creative Potential

1

The Magical Power Within

WE ALL SHARE A profound moment: the day we were born, when we stepped into physical form to embark on our unique journey on this earth. Each of us arrives with immense potential and limitless possibilities, yet at birth, we are entirely unaware of the power we hold within. Many people live their entire lives without ever realizing that they possess the ability to shape their reality and bring their deepest desires to life.

The moment I first became aware of this power was in January 1979, when I attended a keynote address by self-help legend Bob Proctor. Sitting in the audience that evening, I heard Bob share ideas that completely shifted my perspective. He spoke with conviction, saying, "If you can hold it in your mind, you can hold it in your hand." He quoted authors like Vernon Howard, emphasizing, "You cannot escape from a prison if you don't know you're in one." These were concepts I had never encountered before—messages so powerful and transformative that they stirred something deep within me.

That cold January evening marked a turning point in my life. I realized that Bob Proctor had an understanding of life that I did not, and if I truly wanted to escape the emotional pain I was experiencing, I needed to learn from him. But learning isn't enough; transformation requires action. At the end of the event, Bob invited the people in the audience to register for a series of seminars he was leading at a local hotel. Despite my financial struggles and nearly maxed-out credit cards, something inside me—whether intuition or instinct—told me I had to take this step. I needed to invest in myself.

Bob had said something that struck a chord: "If you're not focused on your life getting better, it's getting worse, because nothing stays the same." Those words resonated deeply. I didn't want my life to get worse; I desperately wanted it to improve. So I decided to take a leap of faith, and that decision changed the trajectory of my life forever.

Since that transformative moment, I've been captivated by the principles of manifestation, success, and personal growth. Decades of study, application, and teaching have revealed one undeniable truth: we are all creators, and creation is not a one-time event or a distant memory—it's happening now, in every single moment. Every thought we think, every intention we set, and every feeling we project into the universe contributes to the reality we experience.

Here's the magic: true creation begins when we become aware of this power and deliberately direct it. When we focus our attention, align with our intentions, and embrace the *moment of creation*, everything shifts. Suddenly, life shifts from being a series of random events to a masterpiece of our own making. We stop passively allowing life to unfold and start actively designing it. When we do that, the possibilities are truly endless.

This shift reminds me of a profound truth: "Magic is the opposite of life. With magic, when you know how it works, the magic disappears. But with life, when you know how it works, the magic begins." One of my objectives with this book is to guide you to create magic in your life—real, lasting magic that doesn't fade when you understand how it works but deepens and expands as you master the art of conscious creation.

Understanding the process of creation doesn't diminish its beauty but enhances it. When you know how life works, when you truly grasp the synergy between your thoughts, feelings, and intentions, the magic begins to unfold in ways you may have never imagined. The more you engage with these principles, the more life itself responds, supports, and guides you in extraordinary ways.

The *moment of creation* is a concept that may feel elusive at first, but it's profoundly simple: it is the precise moment when your intentions, thoughts, and feelings come into perfect alignment. This alignment acts as the spark that ignites the process of manifestation. Most people create unconsciously, by default. They dwell on fears, worries, and limitations, inadvertently attracting more of what they *don't* want into their lives.

As the Bible states, "The thing I feared has come upon me" (Job 3:25). This timeless truth reveals the immense power of focus. Whatever we give energy to, whether fear or faith, shapes our reality. Fear functions like a magnet, drawing toward us the very outcomes we wish to avoid. But here's the transformative insight: just as fear can manifest undesirable results, faith, clarity, and intentional focus can create a life filled with abundance, joy, and fulfillment.

When you learn to consciously harness the *moment of creation*, you can shift your energy from fear to faith, from doubt to confidence, and from scarcity to abundance. This is not just a philosophy; it's a practice, and it has the power to change everything.

This principle is not abstract for me. It's a truth I've lived. My journey has been a testament to the power of creation. I've gone from being a struggling single mother with no money to manifesting my dream home, becoming a multimillionaire, and achieving the honor of writing *New York Times* best sellers. My trilogy, *Savy Wisdom*, has even been optioned for a major motion picture, and I've built a global business that has positively impacted millions of lives.

Even during one of the darkest chapters of my life—a diagnosis of metastatic cancer—I relied on the *moment of creation*. Lying in a hospital bed, weakened by radiation treatments, I was faced with a choice: to succumb to fear or to embrace faith. I chose the latter. I focused my mind on the vision of a healthy, vibrant body. I visualized myself as fully healed, strong, and alive, even though my physical reality painted a very different picture.

That experience deepened my understanding of the power of alignment. The moment we align our intentions, thoughts, and feelings, we unlock the ability to transform our circumstances. It's not just a theory: it's a life-altering truth. By focusing on the feelings of perfect health and unwavering faith in my recovery, I invited my body to respond. My healing became a profound testament to the transformative power of the *moment of creation*.

It's important to remember that while the *moment of creation* is immediate—the very second you align your thoughts, feelings, and intentions with your desire—the physical manifestation of your creation often requires time. Just as every seed planted in the earth follows a natural process of growth before it becomes a thriving plant, your desires also have a gestation period. This is not a delay or a denial; it's simply the universe working in perfect harmony with your intention.

The gestation period is where faith plays its most vital role. This is the time to remain steadfast, to continue feeling as though your desire is already here, even when there's no visible evidence of its arrival. It's a time of trust and allowing, knowing that the process is already underway and that what you've created in the unseen will soon be revealed in the seen.

The key is to relax into the knowing that your desire is already on its way, just as you trust that the sun will rise tomorrow. Creation is not about forcing or demanding; it's about aligning, trusting, and allowing. The universe is never late, nor does it make mistakes. The timing of your manifestation will always be perfect, arriving when it is fully ripe and ready to be revealed.

As you step into the next chapter, I invite you to reflect on the desires you hold in your heart right now. Imagine what it would feel like to truly believe they are already yours, to embrace them with gratitude and joy as if they are present in this very moment. This is the essence of creation—the starting point for everything you wish to bring into your life.

As you'll discover in the chapters ahead, this is just the beginning. Together, we'll explore how to deepen your understanding of the creative process, how to remove the blocks that may be holding you back, and how to fully embrace the limitless possibilities that await you.

Creation is happening now, in every moment, whether you are aware of it or not. The beauty of this truth is that the power is already within you—waiting to be tapped, waiting to be directed, waiting to create the life you truly desire.

As you embrace this awareness, you're stepping into the flow of life itself, aligning with a force that is infinite, loving, and always supporting your highest good. Trust in this process and know that the seeds you plant in the *moment of creation* will bloom in their perfect time. Every moment is a new beginning—a chance to choose, to align, and to create.

And the most incredible part? The journey is just as beautiful as the destination. In fact, when you are fully immersed in the *moment of creation*, the journey and the destination become one.

2

The Tug-of-War: Why Alignment Feels Hard

HAVE YOU EVER FELT that you're doing everything right—thinking the right thoughts, visualizing your desires, practicing gratitude—yet nothing seems to be happening? You've taken steps forward, only to feel you've been pulled two steps back. You question whether all the effort is worth it, whether you're on the right path, or worse, whether this whole process even works. I know that feeling. I've been there, more times than I can count.

The struggle to align with your desires is a real and universal experience. It's the internal tug-of-war between what you want and the doubts, fears, and conditioning that keep pulling you back. It's the frustration of looking for evidence of progress and finding none. It's the moment when you start to wonder if you're wasting your time. But in those pivotal, uncomfortable, growth-filled moments the magic of transformation may actually be taking place, even if you can't see it yet.

This chapter is about the struggle. It's about why it feels so hard to get into alignment and, more importantly, to stay there. It's about the invisible barriers we face, the internal battles we fight, and the moments when it feels as if the universe has forgotten us. Most of all, it's about understanding that the struggle and discomfort are a part of the process—and how, with the right tools and perspective, you can move through it with grace and resilience.

As much as I dove headfirst into the study of personal development, I wasn't seeing much change in my life. At the time I didn't realize that the battle that was raging within my own mind. While I was feeding my consciousness valuable, transformative, and insightful new information, the old, deeply embedded programming in my subconscious mind was rejecting these new ideas. It was as if something good was being poured in, only to be blocked because it didn't match the existing patterns.

The Bible says, "In all thy getting, get understanding" (Proverbs 4:7). I was desperate to understand what was happening. For years, I devoured books, listened to audios, attended seminars, and absorbed as much as I could. Although I experienced some emotional shifts, I still felt I was struggling.

Perhaps along the way, someone had explained what might be happening within me—this emotional battle between the new ideas and the old programming—but I was too focused on wanting everything to go right. I wanted the pain to stop. I sought perfection, believing that it would finally bring me peace.

It took years for me to discover that everything was already perfect. Perfect in the here and now. I came to understand that every struggle, every frustration, every moment of feeling stuck was leading me to this exact point in time. The key was to stop seeking and start embracing.

That shift—from striving for perfection to embracing the feeling of perfection in the present moment—was profound. It was as if a weight had been lifted. Faith became my anchor, and I began to trust that everything was working out perfectly, even when it didn't look that way. This realization became a turning point in my journey—a shift in consciousness that changed everything.

It would be dishonest to say that everything fell into place perfectly the moment I realized we create in the present moment. Time and again, I found myself knowing this profound truth, only to lose sight of it and veer off course. The internal struggle was undeniable, but I refused to give up. I realized that if I truly wanted to align with this understanding and see tangible changes in my life, discipline had to become my guiding principle. The practice of discipline enabled a profound shift in my results to take shape.

The struggle to stay in alignment with the *moment of creation* becomes even more challenging when life throws its hardest trials at you. For me, one of the greatest challenges came when I was diagnosed with metastatic cancer. Initially, I approached the treatments with the tools and techniques I had spent years mastering. I focused on visualization, affirming health, and aligning my thoughts with the reality I desired—a healthy, vibrant body.

But as the treatments commenced, things grew progressively harder. My body began to deteriorate, and the side effects of radiation took an unimaginable toll on me. The struggle to maintain alignment, to hold on to faith in the face of relentless physical suffering, felt almost impossible at times.

One oncologist, after assessing my condition during a hospital visit, confirmed that I had radiation poisoning. That diagnosis led to the insertion of a feeding tube and two weeks of hospitalization.

I was confined to a hospital bed, my body weak, and my mind constantly fighting to rise above the pain and fear.

The battle within me was immense. There were moments when I questioned everything—when the evidence around me seemed to contradict every ounce of faith I was trying to hold on to. I had taught myself to believe in the unseen, but how could I maintain that belief when my physical reality was so overwhelmingly bleak? I wondered if the principles I had spent years studying, applying, and teaching even worked. Was I wrong? Was I asking for too much? Was I failing to apply what I knew?

In those darkest moments, I discovered something profound. Even when I felt I was losing the battle, I had a choice. I could choose to dwell in fear, pain, and despair, or I could return, over and over again, to the present moment. To the knowing that creation begins here and now, regardless of the evidence around me. Even when my faith wavered, I found that the simple act of returning—of consciously deciding to focus on health, strength, and gratitude—brought me back into alignment, even if only for a fleeting moment.

I visualized my body healing, strong and vibrant. I embraced the feelings of health and vitality, even as my body told a different story. It wasn't easy: the struggle was real and unrelenting. But this conscious practice of returning to the *moment of creation* allowed me to endure. Slowly but surely, my body began to respond. Each small step forward became evidence that alignment, even in the face of overwhelming struggle, is powerful.

This experience taught me something invaluable: the path of alignment is not always smooth. There will be battles, moments of doubt, and times when everything feels as if it's falling apart. But even in those moments, the power of creation is still within us. We just need to keep returning to it, again and again, until the tide begins to shift.

The struggle for alignment doesn't always appear as life-or-death situations. Sometimes it shows up as the quiet yearning to fulfill a dream, like a desire to do something you've never done before. While the stakes may seem lower, the inner tug-of-war—the doubts, fears, and resistance—can feel just as real. Whether facing physical adversity or simply wrestling with self-doubt, the path to alignment remains the same.

THE LEGACY THAT ALMOST WASN'T

Martha had carried a quiet dream for years—a longing to write a book that would capture the essence of her life's journey. Now that she was in her mid-seventies, the desire flickered in her heart, but just as quickly, doubt crept in like a familiar shadow.

"Maybe I'm not cut out to be a writer. I don't have any talent.

"What difference would it make? Who would even want to read it?

"Maybe it's too late."

The tug-of-war within her mirrored the same internal struggle that many face—the delicate balance between a vision of what could be and the lingering weight of self-doubt.

When Martha came to me, she was unsure if her dream was even worth pursuing. During our first conversation, she voiced her hesitations. I could hear the longing beneath her words, the yearning to create but also the fear of stepping forward.

I asked her a simple question: "What if this book isn't about the masses? What if it's meant for just one person? Would it still be worth writing?"

She paused, and for the first time, I sensed a shift.

One evening, shortly after that call, Martha's granddaughter Emma sat beside her on the living room floor, sifting through old photographs spread across the carpet. Martha recounted stories as they laughed together—tales of love, adventure, and lessons learned along the way. Emma listened intently, soaking in every word as if discovering hidden treasures.

As Martha placed a faded photo back into the box, Emma turned to her and said softly, "Grandma, you should write all of this down. I want to remember your stories someday, and I think others would too."

That simple moment confirmed everything we had discussed.

Martha realized then that her book wasn't meant to sit on store shelves. It wasn't about the size of the audience: it was about the legacy she could leave for the ones who mattered most.

The next morning, Martha opened her notebook for the first time. I guided her through the process, encouraging her to write without worrying about structure or perfection. I told her to imagine she was speaking directly to Emma, pouring her memories and heart onto the pages.

Page by page, Martha's confidence grew. The doubt that once loomed large began to fade. Writing became a joyful ritual, and with each story she told, she felt herself stepping further into alignment—not with the need for recognition, but with the fulfillment of a dream that had long awaited her attention.

When the book was complete, she printed just a few copies—one for Emma, one for each of her children, and one for herself.

Months later, Martha shared the manuscript with me, and I knew right away there was something special about it. I encouraged her to consider publishing it more widely. A local publisher, drawn to the heartfelt simplicity of her words, brought the book to print.

What began as a private legacy for her family found its way into the hands of readers who resonated deeply with Martha's stories. One letter in particular stood out: "Thank you for sharing your life. Your book made me realize that it's not too late for me either."

As Martha read those words, she smiled.

Sometimes the desires that tug at us the longest are the ones with the most purpose. And often the smallest decision to say yes—to begin, to believe—becomes the pivotal moment that changes everything.

3

The Power within the Moment

MOST PEOPLE UNKNOWINGLY SPEND their lives trapped in a relentless cycle, their attention split between two unproductive states: reliving the pain or the regret of the past, or fearing the uncertainty of the future. The past, with its unhealed wounds and mistakes, acts like an anchor, weighing them down with guilt, shame, or sorrow. Meanwhile, the future looms ahead like a dark storm cloud, filled with worries of what-ifs and what might go wrong.

These individuals don't realize that by focusing their energy on these states, they are unknowingly creating more of what they *don't* want. The truth is, whatever you give your attention to—whether it's a painful memory or an imagined fear—becomes your reality. You are feeding those thoughts and feelings with your energy, and in doing so, you're actively shaping your experience, even if you're unaware of it.

But here's the extraordinary part: there's a way out of this cycle. There is a way to harness your power and redirect it. The key lies in one singular, profound realization—creation doesn't happen in the past, nor does it take place in the future. *The only place where creation truly happens is in the present moment.*

This moment, right here and right now, is where your greatest power resides. When you shift your awareness away from the regrets of yesterday and the worries of tomorrow and fully embrace the now, you unlock the infinite potential of creation. It's not about denying the existence of the past or the future; it's about choosing where to focus your energy now.

In this chapter, we'll explore what it means to live in the *moment of creation*, how to recognize when you're truly in alignment, and how to use this awareness to create the life you desire. Once you understand and tap into the power of the present moment, you'll see that it holds the key to everything you've ever wanted.

Adde Murrieta's story is one of profound resilience and unwavering presence. She is a rare example of someone who embodies the art of living in the present moment. Adde has mastered the ability to release anything from the past that doesn't feel good and refuses to allow fear of the future to dictate her life. Her journey is one that deserves to be told, not just because of its extraordinary challenges, but because of the grace, strength, and wisdom with which she overcame them.

At my suggestion, Adde wrote a book about her life experience—a story that reveals the depth of her character and the power of her spirit. She once lived what many would call a picture-perfect life. She was blissfully married, with a beautiful home that felt like a dream come true, three wonderful children, and a future that seemed secure and bright. But life, as it often does, threw her an unthinkable curveball.

One night her entire world came crashing down. At 2:30 a.m., a host of DEA officers, FBI agents, and law enforcement officials broke down her front door and whisked her husband away in handcuffs. Adde was stunned, unable to comprehend what was happening. She soon learned the devastating truth: her husband, the man she had shared her life with for eighteen years, had been dealing drugs—a secret he had kept entirely hidden from her. That night marked the end of what she had believed was a beautiful marriage.

The fallout was swift and merciless. All their assets were frozen, leaving Adde with no financial resources, no job, and three children to care for. It was a situation that could have easily destroyed her. Many would have succumbed to anger, bitterness, and despair. But not Adde.

Rather than allowing this unimaginable betrayal and upheaval to define her, she chose to rise above it. She refused to be buried in grief or paralyzed by anger. Instead, she found the strength to pull herself up, take charge of her life, and rebuild from the ground up. She began to piece together a new life for herself and her children, guided by an inner resilience that is nothing short of extraordinary.

Even now, Adde looks back on that chapter of her life with no regrets. She carries no resentment toward her ex-husband, no bitterness about what was lost. She sees the past for what it is—unchangeable. Adde has a remarkable ability to let go of what no longer serves her and to stay rooted in the present moment. She recognizes that the only thing she can control is how she responds to life's challenges, and she chooses to respond with grace and strength.

Today Adde is remarried to a wonderful man she deeply loves, who cherishes her in return. Together they have built a beautiful life and share two incredible children. They live in a stunning home, and Adde runs her own successful business. Her life may not have been easy, but she chose to take charge and create a life by design rather than a life by defeat.

What makes Adde truly extraordinary is her perspective. While many might be consumed by the pain of betrayal or the fear of an uncertain future, Adde embraces the present moment for the gift that it is. She understands that every moment is an opportunity to start anew, find gratitude, and focus on what can be appreciated. Her story is a testament to the incredible power of the human spirit and the freedom that comes from releasing the past and trusting in the moment.

The more I get to know Adde, the more I realize how rare and inspiring she is. She is a living example of the principles I teach in this book—the power of presence, the courage to release what no longer serves us, and the strength to trust in the possibilities of *now*. Her story is one of transformation, resilience, and the limitless potential that exists within us all when we choose to embrace the present moment.

What does it really mean to live in the *moment of creation* and to embrace this power within? It begins with asking yourself a simple yet profoundly powerful question: *what would I really love?* Whether it's a particular goal, several desires, or the way you choose to live your life, this question is your gateway to creation.

Most people never take the time to ask themselves this question, let alone answer it. They move through life reacting to circumstances, unaware that they hold the power to create their reality. But if you truly understood that you could have anything your heart desires, what would you ask for?

As we journey further into this book, we'll dive deeper into what it means to align fully with your desires—not just to hope or wish but to truly embrace your dreams as though they are already real. For now, let this truth settle in: the moment you decide on a particular outcome, the seed is planted.

Just like a seed in the ground, your desires will manifest when nurtured with faith and the energy of certainty. Creation begins when you accept your desires as already accomplished and align with them in the present moment. The power to manifest lies in your ability to embrace the moment as though your wish is already fulfilled.

4

The Hidden Power of Appreciation

THERE WAS ONCE A man named David who had built a life that, to outsiders, seemed perfect. He had a beautiful wife, Amelia, and a young son, Liam, who adored him. David was successful in his career and proud of the comfortable life he had created for his family. But despite all the blessings surrounding him, David often found himself irritable, impatient, and disconnected from the people he loved most.

Amelia, a gentle and loving woman, bore the weight of his sharp words and distant demeanor. She believed in the power of family and often tried to remind David of the joy found in the little things: Liam's laughter, shared meals, or evening walks. But David rarely acknowledged her efforts. He was caught up in work pressures and personal frustrations, leaving Amelia and Liam feeling invisible in their own home.

Over time, Amelia's heart grew heavy. She began to question whether David even saw the love and care she poured into their family. One evening, after an argument that left Amelia in tears and Liam silent at the dinner table, Amelia made a difficult decision. She packed a small bag and left to stay with her sister, taking Liam with her.

David came home that night to an empty house. At first, he felt angry, frustrated that Amelia had taken such a drastic step. But as the silence settled, he realized how deeply he missed their presence. The weight of absence was heavier than any frustration he had carried.

The next few days were filled with reflection. David began to notice the small details he had overlooked: the warmth Amelia brought to their home, the joy of Liam's playful footsteps echoing in their halls, and the quiet peace of simply being together as a family.

One evening, David sat down with a notebook and began writing a letter to Amelia. Line by line, he poured out his heart, apologizing for the ways he had taken her for granted and acknowledging the love he failed to show. He wrote about his desire to change—to become a husband and father who cherished every moment.

When Amelia returned to collect a few more belongings, David handed her the letter, his eyes full of humility and hope. She read it in silence, tears streaming down her face. After a long pause, she met his gaze and said, "I need to see the change, David. Words aren't enough."

Determined to rebuild what he had nearly lost, David began practicing appreciation every day. Each morning, as he stepped out of bed, he reminded himself to be grateful for his family, his health, and the love that still lingered, waiting to be nurtured. He started small: leaving notes of appreciation for Amelia, playing with Liam even after long workdays, and verbally expressing his gratitude for Amelia's simplest acts of kindness.

Slowly the walls that had formed between them began to dissolve. Amelia noticed David's efforts, and trust gradually returned. One evening, after tucking Liam into bed, David sat next to Amelia on the couch and whispered, "Thank you for giving me another chance."

Amelia smiled softly. "Thank you for seeing what was here all along."

The lesson David learned—and one I wish to extend to you—is that appreciation is one of the most powerful forces of creation. When we express genuine gratitude, we realign ourselves with love, joy, and connection. We become conscious creators, actively shaping the relationships and experiences that define our lives.

No matter where you are on your journey, appreciation can be the spark that reignites the magic you seek. What you focus on grows. Focusing on the blessings already present in your life opens the door for even more abundance to flow.

Take a moment today to reflect on the people and experiences you cherish. Speak your appreciation out loud, write it down, or express it through action. It could be the very thing that shifts your entire world.

5

Manifesting Love: Embracing the Moment with Faith and Feeling

MANIFESTING YOUR DESIRES OFTEN unfolds in the most surprising and unexpected ways. When you come to understand and respect this truth, and when you practice patience, extraordinary things can manifest. For me, the journey of attracting love began with confronting an uncomfortable truth: I had a deeply rooted belief that I was not worthy of love.

This belief, buried in my subconscious, was shaping my experiences. Even when I entered relationships, I would unconsciously sabotage them, blaming my partners without examining my role in the breakdowns. The turning point came when I chose to take an honest look at myself, acknowledging my destructive patterns and deciding to change. Awareness, as I discovered, is the first step toward transformation.

While it isn't always necessary to identify your limiting beliefs in order to manifest your desires, for me this self-reflection was pivotal. Once I recognized the belief holding me back, I made a decision: I was ready to welcome love into my life. Not just any love, but a deep, lasting, joyful, and committed relationship with someone who shared my values—someone for whom family, honesty, and integrity were just as important as they were to me.

With that decision, I began to invest time and energy in visualizing the relationship I wanted. I imagined my soulmate vividly, focusing on his character, values, and the life we would share. In my mind, I created scenes of us traveling together, enjoying family time, celebrating holidays, walking hand in hand through the woods, and sharing intimate meals. I immersed myself in the smells, sounds, tastes, and feelings of those imagined moments, making them as real as possible.

The key to manifestation, and what this book is about, is not just visualizing but feeling as though your desire is already fulfilled. I embraced the feeling of being in love, of having my soulmate by my side, not just in fleeting moments but as my dominant state of being. Whenever doubt or fear crept in, I redirected my focus back to the reality of my desire as though it were already done. While perfection isn't required—none of us can maintain perfect alignment 100 percent of the time—it is essential to hold the feeling as your predominant state.

One of the most liberating aspects of this process is letting go of the *how*. I didn't concern myself with how my soulmate would come into my life. When I shared my intentions with friends, they suggested bars or dating sites. While those are valid options, they didn't resonate with me. Instead, I trusted that the universe would handle the details, knowing that my job was to stay aligned with the feeling of love.

Just two weeks after I made my decision, I experienced something remarkable. While walking my dog around the neighborhood,

I noticed a new neighbor moving in. His dog was tied up on the lawn, and my dog ran over to say hello. That moment brought me face-to-face with a ruggedly handsome man who immediately captured my attention. As we spoke, I felt an undeniable connection. That encounter was the beginning of the most extraordinary relationship of my life. Today I am married to the man of my dreams, and our love grows deeper with each passing day. I often say I won the lottery of love, but the truth is, anyone can. You just have to decide.

My friend Brian Proctor's journey to love is another powerful testament to the process. After years of settling, Brian reached a point where he decided he would no longer compromise. He became crystal clear about what he wanted in a partner and made a firm decision to align with that vision. Like me, Brian had no idea how it would happen, but he focused on feeling as though his ideal relationship already existed.

Brian set a goal: he would be married by his fifty-fifth birthday. Shortly after, he began to recognize his longstanding attraction to a colleague. Despite the physical distance—he lived in Florida, and she was in Alaska—Brian didn't allow logistics to deter him. He took a leap of faith, calling her to express his feelings. Though she hadn't considered him in a romantic light before, his honesty and confidence opened a door.

Over time, their connection deepened. Brian reminded her not to worry about the details, trusting that things would work out. And they did. Less than a year later, just days before Brian's fifty-fifth birthday, they were married in a beautiful ceremony in Hawaii. Today they continue to live their love story, a testament to the power of alignment and faith.

Manifesting love, or any desire, begins with clarity, decision, and alignment. You don't have to know how it will happen; you just have to trust that it will. By staying aligned with the feeling of your desire already fulfilled, you create a powerful energetic state that draws your desires to you.

If you're reading this, know that the process works, not just for me or Brian, but for anyone willing to embrace the present moment with faith and feeling. Decide what you want, align with it, and trust the process. Your manifestation is already in motion.

6

Denying the Evidence of the Senses

THINK ABOUT THIS CONCEPT for a moment: denying the evidence of the senses. What does that truly mean? How does it relate to accessing the *moment of creation*? In a word: *everything*.

One of my clients, Matt, came to me in the middle of what he described as the lowest point in his life. Financially, he was drowning—buried under debt, unable to see a way out, and gripped by constant fear. Every external sign screamed failure.

Matt had no idea how he would turn his life around. He told me that every attempt he made to improve his circumstances seemed to fall apart before he gained any real traction. The evidence in front of him painted a grim picture.

But during one of our conversations, I could sense a flicker of determination beneath the doubt. I told him plainly: "I know you can do this. I believe in you."

At first, Matt dismissed it. "That's easy for you to say," he replied. But after a pause, he added something I'll never forget: "You know what? I have nothing left to lose. I don't have anything now, so I can't fall any further. Maybe I'll just borrow your belief until I find my own."

That was his turning point.

Despite the overwhelming evidence around him—his empty bank account, the bills piling up, and the absence of immediate opportunities—Matt decided to persist. Every day, he committed to visualizing abundance, even when his reality showed none. He leaned into the belief I held for him, returning to it whenever doubt crept back in.

Weeks turned into months, and while external results didn't appear right away, Matt stayed the course. Then, unexpectedly, he received a job opportunity that aligned with his skills—one he hadn't even applied for. That job paved the way for a consulting project, which eventually grew into a thriving business.

Matt later told me that had he relied solely on the evidence of his senses, he would have quit long before that first opportunity appeared.

His breakthrough didn't come from perfect conditions or a lucky break. It came from the simple but powerful decision to deny the appearance of lack and hold faith, even when it felt impossible.

Most people live their lives based on what they can see, hear, touch, taste, or smell. They allow their external circumstances to dictate their emotions, thoughts, and decisions. If the bank account is low, they choose to feel despair. If a bill arrives, they choose to feel overwhelmed. If they're struggling in a relationship, they may feel hopeless. The problem is that this kind of living is reactive, not creative. It keeps people trapped in a cycle where they only respond to what is, rather than creating what could be. Emotions can become habitual, but developing the awareness to recognize what you are feeling and consciously choosing to disengage from that emotion, replacing it with a more empowering one, is a profoundly productive and positive practice.

Living in this reactive state is like driving a car while staring in the rearview mirror. If your focus is always on the past—on past struggles, failures, or betrayals—you're bound to crash. It's not the way to drive, or the way to move forward. It's dangerous and, frankly, counterproductive. Similarly, if you're gripped by fear of the future—whether it's fear of financial ruin, rejection, or failure—those fears will shape your reality. Why? Because what you focus on expands.

This is the fundamental truth that most people miss: your current reality is not a reflection of what's possible—it's simply a reflection of your past thoughts, beliefs, and emotions. If you want to create something new, you have to break free from the grip of the senses and shift your focus to what you truly desire. You must live as though the reality you want is already here, even when there's no physical evidence to support it.

Fear is one of the most powerful emotions that keeps people stuck in a cycle of struggle. Whether it's fear of not having enough money, losing what they have, or never achieving their dreams, this emotion can paralyze even the most ambitious individuals. Fear, when left unchecked, becomes a self-fulfilling prophecy.

Let's use money as an example. Like Matt, many people live with a constant fear of not having enough. They focus on their debts, their bills, or the seemingly endless expenses that pile up. This fear creates a powerful emotional charge that reinforces the very reality they're trying to escape. Remember, the universe doesn't respond to what you want; it responds to the energy you emit. If your dominant energy is fear or lack, you will attract more situations that reinforce those feelings.

But what if you could shift that energy? What if, instead of focusing on the fear of not having enough, you focused on gratitude for what you do have? What if you began to feel abundant, even when your external circumstances didn't yet reflect abundance?

This is what it means to deny the evidence of the senses. It's about choosing to align your thoughts and emotions with your desired reality, not your current reality.

Another one of my clients came to me overwhelmed by financial stress. She had accumulated a significant amount of debt—more than six figures—and felt completely trapped. She was consumed by thoughts of fear and failure. Every time she opened her mailbox, she felt a wave of panic, knowing another bill was waiting for her. She told me she couldn't sleep at night because her mind was racing with worry about how she would pay her creditors. Her fear was so intense that it began to affect her health and relationships.

When she approached me for help, the first thing I told her was this: "Your financial situation will not change until your mindset does. Right now, you're letting your financial situation control you and giving it too much power."

She looked at me skeptically, as though I hadn't heard a word about her overwhelming debt. But I assured her that no matter how dire her external circumstances seemed, the real issue wasn't the debt itself—it was her emotional and energetic relationship with it.

I asked her to start by getting clear on the life she truly wanted. What would it feel like to be debt-free? What would she do with her money if she had more than enough? What would financial freedom mean to her? At first, she struggled to imagine it. Her mind kept pulling her back to her current reality, to the fear and worry she knew so well. But with practice, she began to shift. She wrote out a detailed vision of her financially abundant life and recorded it as a Power Life Script®—a tool I developed to help people reprogram their subconscious minds.

I encouraged her to listen to this script multiple times a day, especially during moments when her fears resurfaced. At night, when her mind tried to replay her worries, she would put on her script and let the words guide her into a state of calm and confidence. I also taught her a simple but powerful practice: whenever she felt overwhelmed by a bill or financial obligation, she would pause, take a deep breath, and say, "I am grateful for the abundance in my life."

Over time, her mindset began to shift. She started to see money not as a source of stress, but as a tool for creating the life she wanted. She became less reactive to her circumstances and more focused on her vision.

As her energy shifted, so did her reality. Within two years, she had paid off her debts, increased her income significantly, and built a financial cushion that gave her peace of mind. The transformation was remarkable, but it all started with one decision: to deny the evidence of the senses and focus on the reality she wanted to create.

In 1995, after my divorce, I faced one of the most challenging financial situations of my life. I was determined to buy a home for myself and my son, even though I had no savings and no clear plan for how I would afford it. But I made a decision: I would own that home. I visualized it in detail—the layout of the rooms, the smell of the fresh paint, the sound of my son laughing as he played in the yard. I felt the emotions of owning it as though it were already mine. Most importantly, I gave thanks for it every single day.

At the time, there was no logical reason to believe I could pull it off. My bank account told one story, but my faith told another. I refused to let fear or doubt take over. I focused only on the outcome I wanted, and I acted as though it were already done. Within months, the funds I needed materialized, and I was able to purchase the home. It was one of the most profound experiences of my life, and it taught me an invaluable lesson: the universe always finds a way when you align your energy with your desire.

Manifestation isn't just about thinking positive thoughts—it's about feeling as though your desire is already here. Emotions are the fuel of creation. If you want to manifest abundance, you must feel abundant. If you want to manifest love, you must feel loved. If you want to manifest success, you must feel successful. This doesn't mean ignoring your current circumstances or pretending they don't exist. It means choosing to focus your energy on what you want, not what you don't want. It means living in the present moment with faith and gratitude, knowing that your desires are already here.

By denying the evidence of the senses and aligning your energy with your desires, you have the power to transform your reality. The process takes practice and patience, but the results are life-changing. In the latter part of the book, we'll dive into the most effective tools and techniques to help you deepen your alignment, accelerate your manifestations, and set yourself up for success with ease.

7

Transforming Emotional Habits for Success

HAVE YOU EVER FOUND yourself reacting to a situation in a way that feels automatic, almost as if you're on autopilot? Perhaps you've noticed certain emotions arise repeatedly—frustration, anger, sadness, or unworthiness. These patterns, these habitual emotions, often run so deep that we fail to question them, let alone recognize where they come from. Yet our emotions are not just fleeting moments; they are habits, deeply ingrained in our subconscious minds, and they shape the way we experience the world.

Much like thoughts, emotions can become habitual. When we experience a specific emotion repeatedly in response to certain triggers, it forms a groove in our subconscious mind—a default reaction that becomes automatic over time. Without realizing it, we begin to live in these emotions, reacting the same way over and over again. Most people are unaware of these patterns and the grip they have on their lives.

Take my own story. For years, I had a habit of anger. It didn't matter whether the situation was big or small: anger would erupt almost instantly. If someone cut me off in traffic, I'd feel a surge of irritation, as if that small act of carelessness was a personal attack. My first husband once pointed out that I tended to magnify negative emotions, turning small stones into giant boulders. It wasn't until I began to study and consciously reflect on my emotions that I realized this habit of anger stemmed from my childhood. Growing up in an abusive environment, I developed anger as a defense mechanism. But that habitual emotion no longer served me as an adult. It controlled me.

Once I became aware of this pattern, I also noticed how seemingly insignificant triggers—like witnessing a parent scolding their child in a grocery store—would evoke that same automatic anger. It wasn't about the moment itself; it was about the unresolved emotional habit ingrained in my subconscious.

Here's the key: emotions, no matter how habitual, can be reprogrammed. But first we must notice them.

Awareness is the first step toward transformation. Without awareness, we remain blind to our patterns, reacting without questioning why. Many of my clients have experienced profound breakthroughs simply by choosing to be aware of their emotions.

One client in particular had a deep-rooted habit of feeling unworthy. She shared how small, everyday interactions would trigger her sense of insignificance—whether it was being overlooked by a customer service representative or feeling excluded from social plans. She would dwell on these moments, using them as proof to validate her unworthiness. Over time, this habit of seeking evidence for her perceived lack of value compounded, creating a belief system that kept her stuck.

When we sat down to address this issue, I asked her to begin an awareness journal. Following my guidance, she drew a line down the center of a page and labeled one column "Positive Thoughts/Feelings" and the other "Negative Thoughts/Feelings." Each day, she noted when she felt a surge of positive or negative emotion and identified what triggered it. It didn't take long for her to notice her patterns. She began to see how often she defaulted to feelings of unworthiness and how frequently she sought external validation for those feelings.

It is essential to understand that all emotions are generated within us. Emotions do not come from external people, circumstances, or events: they are an expression of our internal state. We often think, "This person made me feel unworthy," or, "That situation caused my anger." But the reality is, emotions originate within us. They are our responses to what we perceive, not something we "get" from others.

Take the feeling of worthiness. Many people believe that their sense of worth is tied to external validation—compliments, recognition, or approval from others. But worthiness is not something that anyone else can give you. It's an inside job. If you want to feel worthy, you must decide to feel worthy. You must embody the emotion of worthiness within yourself, independent of anyone else's actions or opinions.

This is why the process of rewiring emotional habits is so empowering. It puts the control back in your hands. Instead of looking outward for someone or something to make you feel a certain way, you begin to cultivate and express those emotions from within. You take responsibility for your emotional state, and in doing so, you reclaim your power.

But awareness alone is not enough. To truly change, you must act on that awareness. You must consciously choose a different response.

Let's go back to my habit of anger. Once I became aware of it, I made a conscious decision to change. The next time a car cut me off, instead of reacting with irritation, I chose to pause, smile, and say to myself, "Isn't that interesting? That person must be in a hurry, or perhaps they didn't see me." Then I sent them a silent wish of goodwill. That simple shift from anger to indifference—and even kindness—was incredibly liberating. It didn't happen overnight, but with consistent effort, I rewired that emotional habit.

The same applies to any habitual emotion, whether it's unworthiness, fear, or guilt. When you notice the pattern, choose to respond differently. Create a new thought that leads to a better feeling. Over time, this deliberate act of choosing will create a new emotional habit—one that supports and uplifts you.

Let me be clear: changing emotional habits is not easy. These patterns have often been with us for years, sometimes decades. They are deeply rooted in our subconscious, and breaking free from them requires discipline, effort, and patience.

When my client committed to rewriting her habit of unworthiness, it was a daily practice. Each time she felt a pang of insignificance, she chose to switch her focus. If she felt overlooked, she reminded herself of her inherent value and expressed gratitude for the people who loved and appreciated her. If she felt envious of someone else's success, she shifted to appreciation, celebrating their achievement instead of resenting it. Slowly but surely, she began to rewire her emotional patterns.

I often remind my clients that emotions, like muscles, are strengthened with use. The more you practice a particular emotion, the stronger it becomes. If you constantly dwell in fear or doubt, those emotions will dominate your experience. But if you practice gratitude, joy, and faith, those emotions will grow and shape your reality.

Habits of emotion are not bound by age. They can deepen and solidify over time if we allow them to, becoming the default way we express ourselves. My father was a perfect example of this. He was a grumpy man, often short-tempered and irritable. As he got older, it seemed as though his grumpiness only intensified.

It wasn't until he suffered a stroke and was diagnosed with dementia that something extraordinary happened: he became sweet, childlike, and gentle. My aunt, his sister, told me, "This is the Bobby I remember as a child." She shared how, when he was young, he was playful, kind, and full of life. Somewhere along the way, however, he developed the habit of being grumpy. Life's challenges, disappointments, or circumstances had shaped his emotional patterns, and grumpiness became his default state.

This story highlights something important: emotional habits can take root over time and, if unchecked, can harden into character. Many elderly individuals, like my father, may find themselves stuck in such patterns. Old-age homes can sometimes feel as if they're filled with grumpy seniors. They're grumpy not because they have to be, but because they've unknowingly strengthened those emotional habits over a lifetime.

The good news is that it's never too late to change. Even the grumpiest among us can decide to shift their emotional patterns. It takes awareness, effort, and the willingness to do the work. Imagine what it would feel like for someone who has been habitually grumpy to choose joy, playfulness, or gratitude instead. The transformation might seem small at first, but over time, it could reshape not only their experience of life but also their relationships with those around them.

This story of my father is a reminder that no matter how ingrained an emotional habit may seem, it's never permanent. The power to change always resides within us. Whether we are young or old, the decision to choose a better emotional habit and follow through with the necessary work can lead to profound change.

Habits of emotion are formed through our own experiences, but they are also learned through observation, especially in childhood. My father, as I mentioned, had a habit of being grumpy. While I don't believe for a second that he or my mother ever intended to teach us to be angry or irritable, children naturally absorb the behaviors and emotional patterns of their parents. Parents are, after all, their children's first and most influential role models.

Looking back, I realize that some of my own habits of anger may have stemmed from what I observed growing up. My parents both worked tirelessly to provide for us, and life was often filled with struggle and stress. In moments of frustration or exhaustion, their emotions would naturally surface, and as children, we were there to witness it all. While they were doing their best (as all parents do), they were unknowingly modeling certain emotional responses to life's challenges.

As children, we are like sponges. We take in what we see, hear, and feel, and we begin to internalize it. If a child frequently observes a parent becoming easily angered or irritated, they might adopt similar emotional patterns without even realizing it. It's not that the parents set out to teach anger or frustration; it's simply what the child perceives as a normal or acceptable way of responding to the world.

This is not about placing blame on parents—far from it. Parenting is one of the most challenging roles in life, and no parent is perfect. But it does highlight the importance of awareness. As adults, we have the ability to reflect on our emotional habits and trace them back to their origins. In doing so, we can begin to separate the patterns we inherited from the ones we wish to cultivate moving forward.

Recognizing this connection can also help parents today. By becoming aware of their own emotional habits, they can choose to model healthier patterns for their children. Imagine a child growing up in a home where joy, patience, and gratitude are the dominant emotions. Those emotional habits would likely shape their view of the world in a far more positive way.

For me, becoming aware of how I may have learned anger allowed me to take responsibility for changing it. Once I noticed the pattern, I could make the conscious decision to shift to emotions that aligned more with the life I wanted to create. This choice is available to everyone, regardless of their past.

Discipline is the foundation for lasting change. Emotional habits are like well-worn paths in the brain: creating a new path takes time and consistent effort. But each time you choose a better thought, each time you switch to a positive emotion, you strengthen that new path. Eventually, that new way of being becomes your default.

The beauty of this work is that it's not about perfection. It's about progress. Each moment offers a new opportunity to choose again, to align with emotions that uplift and empower you. As you do, you'll find that the world around you begins to shift in remarkable ways.

By recognizing and rewiring your emotional habits, you reclaim your power. You step into the *moment of creation* with intention and clarity, shaping a life that reflects the best of who you are. And that, my friend, is a habit worth cultivating.

TOOLS FOR REWIRING EMOTIONAL HABITS

To support this process, I encourage you to adopt tools that help you stay conscious and intentional:

Awareness journaling. Begin by tracking your emotions and identifying triggers. This simple practice will illuminate your patterns and help you understand the root of your habitual emotions.

Reframing thoughts. When a negative emotion arises, pause and reframe the thought that triggered it. Replace it with a thought that evokes a positive emotion.

Daily visualization. Spend a few minutes each day visualizing yourself as the person you want to be—calm, confident, joyful. Feel the emotions of that version of yourself as if it's already who you are.

Affirmations. Use positive affirmations to reinforce new beliefs. For example, if you struggle with unworthiness, repeat affirmations like, "I am deserving of love and abundance."

Celebrate progress. Acknowledge even the smallest shifts in your emotional patterns. Celebrate your growth, and stay patient with yourself.

8

The Immediate Manifestation

WHEN YOU ACCEPT YOUR desires into your heart as an accomplished fact, they are done. Where are they done? you might ask. They are done in the fourth dimension—your imagination. All manifestations are first created in this invisible space, the realm of infinite possibilities, before they materialize in the physical world.

One of the most rapid and fulfilling manifestations I've ever experienced was becoming a PhD graduate—something I hadn't even considered until I was sixty-five years old.

For most of my life, the idea of pursuing higher education wasn't even on my radar. I had barely made it through high school, and at the time, I felt that school was more of an inconvenience than a stepping stone. I never earned a college degree, and for the longest time, I held the belief that it wasn't necessary for me. But at sixty-five, something shifted.

The desire to pursue a PhD emerged almost out of nowhere. I can't say I had been planning it, but when the thought crossed my mind, I felt an immediate spark—as if it was already part of my future. I knew from decades of studying the mind and manifestation that if I wanted this, the first step wasn't about figuring out the logistics. It was about embodying the mindset of someone who already held a PhD.

That's exactly what I did. I began to think, feel, and act as though I had already achieved the degree. I visualized the certificate in my hand, imagined what it would feel like to write "Dr." before my name, and adopted the energy of someone deeply immersed in advanced study.

Before long, opportunities began to align. I found the perfect university, enrolled, and moved through each stage—earning my bachelor's, then a master's, and finally completing my PhD in philosophy with a specialization in metaphysical science.

The most remarkable part of the journey was how natural it felt. There was no struggle, no second-guessing. I decided early on that this process would be smooth and enjoyable, and it was. Every exam, every paper, every thesis and dissertation felt like a natural extension of who I was. In fact, I looked forward to the work, knowing it was reinforcing everything I had studied and taught for decades.

When I held that degree in my hand, it felt like the final piece of a 5,000-piece puzzle clicking into place. It wasn't just about the title; it was about the clarity and completeness it brought to my life's work. The process deepened my understanding of metaphysics, strengthened my belief in what's possible, and solidified everything I had been teaching.

Reflecting on this experience, I know it stands as a powerful example of what can happen when you align your mind and emotions with a desire—when you step into the identity of the person you wish to become before the physical manifestation occurs.

Manifestation doesn't have to take years. Sometimes it's simply about deciding that the process will be easy and allowing it to unfold with joy and confidence.

After I had written eighteen nonfiction books, one of my team members asked me to record a video on how I had written my first fiction book. At first, I thought it was an odd request. I had spent years teaching authors—both fiction and nonfiction—how to write, publish, and succeed, but I had never actually written a fiction book myself. That suggestion sparked a simple but powerful question: "Do I want to write a fiction book?" The answer came instantly—yes. I knew I wanted to, and I felt the excitement of possibility immediately flood in.

The next question I asked myself was: "What do I need to believe and focus on in order to write a great book?" I realized that I needed to believe I could do it, that the process would be easy, and that the book would be extraordinary. Within minutes, I made the decision to write my first fiction book. I called it *Savy Wisdom*, and it went on to become one of my most successful books to date. The creative process unfolded effortlessly, and I enjoyed every moment of writing it. That single decision aligned me with the outcome I desired, and as a result, the words flowed through me with ease. Writing *Savy Wisdom* was not only fulfilling but deeply enjoyable.

The success of that book led to two sequels, creating a trilogy. I eventually sold the rights to the trilogy to be made into a motion picture. Reflecting on that experience, I realized that the key to such immediate manifestation was alignment. The moment I decided it would be easy, it was. The moment I believed in the outcome, the results began to take shape. Manifestation often begins with a single decision—a moment of clarity and unwavering belief.

Let's do an exercise. Take a moment to think about something you deeply desire—a goal, a dream, or an accomplishment that fills your heart with excitement. It could be a thing, like a dream home or luxury car. It could be an experience, like earning an award, completing a marathon, or building a loving relationship. Or it could be financial, like reaching a specific income or net worth.

With that desire in mind, imagine it as if it already exists in your life. Picture yourself saying, "Now that I am easily earning $_____, I feel relaxed and abundant." Or, "Now that I'm living in my beautiful home, I feel joyful and grateful." Close your eyes and feel the emotions of having it—right now. Let yourself feel the peace, the joy, the excitement, the love. That moment, right there, is the *moment of creation*.

You are creating in every moment, whether you're aware of it or not. Most people, however, walk through life entirely unconscious of what they're creating. They allow their thoughts and emotions to run on autopilot, often focusing on fears, doubts, or frustrations, and unintentionally attract more of the same.

Accepting your desire into your heart is simple, but sustaining that acceptance can be a challenge. Why? Because our minds are programmed by years—sometimes decades—of beliefs, patterns, and habits that contradict the idea of having what we want. When there is no physical evidence to support your new reality, doubt and fear may creep in. It takes discipline, repetition, and unwavering faith to stay aligned with the emotions of your desire as already accomplished.

When I decided to become an author, I didn't just imagine writing books: I visualized myself as a successful author who was making a positive difference in the lives of others. I saw my books on best-seller lists, imagined receiving heartfelt messages from readers, and felt the immense joy of knowing my work was making an impact. At first, it felt strange—almost unnatural—but I persisted. Over time, this became my reality.

Setting the audacious goal of becoming a *New York Times* bestselling author was a stretch for me. But through consistent visualization and emotional alignment, it happened. The process of acceptance and continual engagement with the feeling of the desire created that outcome.

One of my clients came to me with a dream of building a successful coaching business. She wanted to earn millions of dollars annually and make a meaningful impact on women's lives. Together, we worked on creating a clear vision.

I asked her, "How will you know when you're successful?" She described her dream in vivid detail—earning $5 million annually, empowering women, living in her dream home, giving generously, and creating investments. I encouraged her to embrace the feelings of already having achieved it. What would she feel like? What would she do with her earnings? What would her daily life look like?

She embraced the process wholeheartedly, scripting her life as if she were already living it and immersing herself in gratitude for her accomplishments. Within a few years, her dream became her reality. She now earns millions annually and has become a well-known figure in the personal development industry.

The secret? She lived in the *moment of creation*, repeatedly feeling and believing in her success until it manifested.

This process may sound simple, but for those who are not yet in the habit, it can feel foreign or even difficult. The good news is that it gets easier with practice. You are building habits of success.

I've used this process to manifest everything from dream homes to luxury vacations, from financial abundance to deeply meaningful relationships. I've manifested my soulmate husband, Denis, with whom I share a beautiful marriage. I've manifested a successful business that has thrived for decades. I've manifested a *New York Times* best seller and even the adaptation of my fiction trilogy into a movie.

The Universal Process of Manifestation

The process of manifestation is the same for any desire.
- Decide what you want. Be clear and specific.
- Determine what it feels like to have it. Emotions are the key to alignment.
- Feel it every day as your dominant way of being.
- Go straight to the feeling. Immerse yourself in the emotions of already having your desire.

Manifestation is not a random act of luck: it's a deliberate and repeatable process. It works for anything you desire.

The hardest part is not the initial act of imagining your desire but maintaining the emotional state of its fulfillment. When doubt or fear arises, the key is to notice it, release it, and return to the feeling of gratitude and accomplishment. Remember, you are the creator of your reality. Every moment is a new opportunity to realign with your desires and create anew.

In the next chapter, we'll explore how to overcome common challenges that arise on the journey to manifestation and how to stay aligned with your vision, no matter what external circumstances may appear.

9

Rising above Challenges

CHALLENGES ARE AN INEVITABLE part of life. No matter how meticulously you plan or how much effort you put into creating the life you desire, obstacles will arise. They come in many forms—financial setbacks, health issues, relationship struggles, unexpected losses—but they all have one thing in common: they present us with an opportunity. An opportunity to grow, to learn, and to rise above.

Sometimes the most transformative moments are hidden within the experiences we least expect—or want. My sister's journey is a testament to that.

In 2009, she was caught in a massive layoff at the multinational corporation where she had worked for years. Up until that day, her entire career had been in corporate environments. When she called me from the parking lot, holding her layoff letter and personal belongings, she was understandably shaken. Not only had she lost her job, but she was also the primary breadwinner, supporting her household.

I'll never forget what I told her in that moment. "This is wonderful," I said. "Now you can start your own business."

At the time, she didn't share my enthusiasm. The idea of framing the situation as "wonderful" felt almost absurd to her. But my words made her pause. That tiny interruption in her thought process planted a seed.

Although she had no experience running her own business, she decided to take the leap. Within weeks, she had shifted her mindset from fear to possibility. That single decision changed the trajectory of her life. Her business began to thrive, and to this day she continues to work from home doing what she loves—something she may have never pursued had she not been laid off.

A few years later, life dealt her another unimaginable challenge. Her husband—her soulmate—was diagnosed with cancer and passed away within months. She was devastated. They had built a life of love and happiness together, and his passing left a deep void.

Even in her grief, she found the courage to dream again. She shared with me her desire to own a second home in Florida, but when I encouraged her to go for it, she responded, "I'm not you."

I asked her one simple question: "Do you want the home?"

"Yes," she said quietly.

"Then I can help you get it," I replied.

Days later, she purchased a brand-new home on a beautiful lake. It was everything she had imagined and more. That home became a place of joy and peace for her, a sanctuary during a time of healing.

Her story stands as a reminder that life doesn't wait for the perfect moment. It doesn't pause until you feel ready. Sometimes it takes the unexpected—the job loss, the heartbreak, the uncertainty—to awaken something greater within us.

In our darkest moments, we can choose to rise—not just to overcome but to create something extraordinary.

It's not the challenges themselves that define us, but how we respond to them. Our greatest power lies in our ability to choose—to choose how we think, how we feel, and how we act, even in the face of adversity. Rising above challenges requires a mindset of resilience, a heart full of faith, and the discipline to stay aligned with your vision, no matter what storms may come.

Life is unpredictable, and challenges are a part of the human experience. They are neither punishment nor evidence of failure; they are simply part of the journey. Yet so many people see challenges as roadblocks, as reasons to give up. They ask, "Why me?" or "What did I do to deserve this?" Instead, the question we should be asking is, "What do I choose now/next?" or "How will I grow from this?"

One of the most profound lessons I've learned in my journey is that challenges are not meant to break us—they are meant to build us. They force us to dig deep, to discover strengths we didn't know we had, and to develop qualities like patience, courage, and perseverance.

When I was diagnosed with metastatic cancer in 2021, it felt as if the ground had been pulled out from under me. I had spent decades studying and teaching personal growth, and here I was, faced with one of the greatest challenges of my life. At that moment, I had a choice: I could succumb to fear and despair, or I could rise above. I chose to rise.

Rising above didn't mean denying the reality of my situation. It meant choosing how I would respond to it. I focused on aligning my thoughts with health, imagining my body as whole and vibrant. I practiced gratitude for the doctors and treatments available to me.

Even on the hardest days, I reminded myself that this challenge was not the end of my story—it was a chapter that would lead to growth and transformation.

Every challenge carries a gift, though it may not be immediately apparent. Often it is only in hindsight that we see how a difficult experience shaped us for the better. Think back to a challenge you've faced in your own life. At the time, it may have felt overwhelming or unfair. But looking back, can you see how it strengthened you? Can you see how it taught you something valuable?

When I went through my divorce in 1995, it was one of the most painful experiences of my life. I was a single mother with no savings and no clear path forward. But that challenge taught me resilience. It taught me how to rely on my inner strength and how to create a vision for a better future, even when my current circumstances seemed bleak. During that time, I began to truly understand the power of alignment and manifestation.

Challenges also have a way of revealing what's truly important. They strip away the superficial and force us to focus on what matters most—our health, our relationships, our inner peace. They remind us of the strength we carry within and the limitless potential we have to create a life of joy and fulfillment, no matter the circumstances.

Rising above challenges requires more than just willpower; it requires tools and practices that help you stay aligned with your vision. Here are some of the tools that have helped me and my clients navigate life's storms:

Reframe the challenge. Shift your perspective by asking empowering questions. Instead of "Why is this happening to me?" ask, "What do I choose to learn from this?" or "How will this make me stronger?"

Embrace faith and gratitude. Even in the darkest moments, there is always something to be grateful for. Gratitude shifts your focus from what's wrong to what's right, creating a positive vibration that attracts solutions and opportunities.

Visualize the outcome. Stay focused on the result you desire, not the problem at hand. Imagine yourself on the other side of the challenge, feeling proud and accomplished.

Take aligned action. Challenges often require action, but not all actions are created equal. Take steps that are aligned with your vision and your values. Trust your intuition to guide you.

Practice patience. Remember that every challenge has a gestation period. Trust the process and give yourself grace as you navigate the journey.

Surround yourself with support. You don't have to face challenges alone. Lean on your support system—friends, family, mentors, or a mentor. Sometimes just having someone to listen can make all the difference.

As I reflect on my own life, I am struck by how many of my greatest accomplishments were born out of challenges. My career as a *New York Times* best-selling author began as a dream during a time when I was struggling financially. My beautiful marriage to Denis came after years of heartbreak and self-discovery. Even my journey with cancer, as difficult as it was, deepened my faith and strengthened my resolve to live a life of purpose and joy.

I share this not to say that challenges are easy—they're not. But they are opportunities for growth, transformation, and stepping into the best version of ourselves. Every challenge you face is a chance to rise, become stronger, and create a life that reflects your highest potential.

The most powerful tool for rising above challenges is the present moment. Challenges often pull us into the past, where we dwell on what went wrong, or into the future, where we fear what might happen. But the present moment is where your power lies. It's where you can choose your thoughts, align with your vision, and take inspired action.

No matter what challenge you're facing, know that you have the power to rise above. You are stronger than you think, and the tools to overcome are already within you. Trust in the process, lean into your resilience, and remember that every challenge is an opportunity to create something extraordinary.

This moment—this very moment—is your *moment of creation*. What will you choose to create?

10

The Universe Always Has Your Back

IMAGINE HAVING A PARTNER so powerful, resourceful, and loyal that no matter what you ask for, they deliver. This partner doesn't judge you, criticize you, or place conditions on what you can or cannot have. They simply respond to your energy, your feelings, and your beliefs. They are your unwavering ally, always working behind the scenes to bring your desires into reality.

That partner is the Universe. Some call it God, Buddha, Allah, the Holy Spirit, Jehovah, or another sacred name. What you call it doesn't matter: an unseen power is always available to you. In this book, we'll refer to it as the Universe.

The Universe is the ultimate collaborator in the creation of your life. It operates in perfect harmony with the laws of energy, vibration, and attraction. It's always at work, responding to the signals you send through your thoughts, emotions, and alignment. And the most incredible truth? This partner is available to every single one of us—right here, right now.

Here's the key: just like any relationship, your partnership with the Universe requires trust, faith, and effort on your part. You have a role to play, and the Universe has its role too. When you understand this dynamic and step fully into your part, the Universe moves mountains to meet you.

Think of your relationship with the Universe as similar to driving an electric vehicle. You must first plug it in. Without that connection, there's no charge, no energy to fuel the vehicle. In the same way, for the Universe to work its magic, you must "plug in" through your alignment, faith, and focus.

Your role is to be clear about what you desire, align your energy with the feelings of already having it, and trust that the Universe is orchestrating everything perfectly. You don't need to figure out the *how*—that's the Universe's job. Your job is to stay connected, maintain your alignment, and relax in knowing that your desire is already here.

This is where many people struggle. They get impatient, doubtful, or fearful when they don't see immediate evidence of their desires. They start to question whether the Universe is really working for them. But let me remind you of this simple truth: the Universe is always at work. Even when you can't see it, even when it doesn't feel like it, the wheels are turning in your favor.

The Universe doesn't judge, criticize, or condemn. It doesn't analyze whether your desires are "good" or "bad." It simply responds to your dominant emotions and beliefs. Your emotions act as a magnetic pull, drawing to you experiences that match your energetic vibration.

Imagine the Universe as a silent, ever-present mentor—always listening to your thoughts, paying attention to your every feeling, and being deeply aware of the energy you emit. It responds the energy you direct toward your desires. If you could truly imagine that someone, or something, was observing your every thought and noticing your every emotion, how would you choose to direct your energy? Would you focus on what you truly desire, or would you let doubt, fear, and frustration take over?

When you shift your focus to what you truly want, you become aligned with the force that is waiting to bring it to you.

If your dominant emotion is joy, the Universe says yes and sends you more reasons to feel joyful. If your dominant emotion is fear, the Universe also says yes and sends you experiences that align with that fear. The Universe is a mirror, reflecting back to you the energy you put out into the world. This one shift in perspective changed everything for me: it made me more aware of where I was consciously giving my attention.

This is why alignment is so important. When you align with the emotions of already having your desire—gratitude, joy, love—the Universe mirrors those emotions back to you in the form of manifestations. The process is simple, but it requires you to take responsibility for your energy and your emotions.

One of the biggest challenges people face is trusting the process. It's easy to feel impatient, especially when you don't see immediate results. But think of it this way: when you order a meal at a restaurant, you don't run into the kitchen and demand to know when your food will be ready. You place your order, trust that it's being prepared, and relax while you wait.

The same principle applies to the Universe. When you align with your desire and send your "order" out into the Universe, your role is to relax in the knowing that it is done. Trust that the Universe is preparing everything in perfect timing, in the most miraculous and harmonious way.

In 1995, while going through one of the most challenging transitions of my life—divorce and single motherhood—I made a decision that many would have called reckless. I decided to buy my dream home, even though I didn't have the funds to do it.

At the time, my previous husband and I were trying to sell our shared home. The real estate market was sluggish, and despite lowering the price twice, we had no offers. I could have let that discourage me, but I didn't. I held tight to the vision of owning a beautiful home for myself and my toddler son.

I visualized it. I felt it. I trusted that it was already mine.

One day I walked into a model home that took my breath away. It was stunning, and something inside me just knew that it was mine. I visualized living in it in vivid detail—the layout of the furniture in the rooms, the view from the windows, the feeling of walking through the front door. I decided to purchase it, although I didn't have the money to cover the cost.

I placed the deposit using a cash advance on my Visa card. Now let me be clear: this isn't financial advice I'd give to anyone else. But in that moment, it was the only way I could see to move forward. The deposit wasn't large, just a couple of thousand dollars, but it allowed me to secure the home.

At the time, there wasn't a requirement to prove that I had all the funds to pay for the house upfront. I was relying entirely on faith, and honestly, I had no idea how I would cover the closing costs.

As fate would have it, I had recently begun working for the very first Internet start-up in the country. One of the perks of my employment was the opportunity to purchase nonrestricted shares in the company. The company was planning an IPO (initial public offering), but the timing of it was distant. At least that's what I thought.

In an incredible twist of serendipity, the company went public just four days before the closing date on my house. Not only did the IPO launch successfully, but the stock value soared. I suddenly found myself with all the money I needed to cover the purchase—right on the day I needed it most.

It was a close call, but everything aligned perfectly.

This experience taught me something invaluable: the Universe is always conspiring in our favor, even when we can't see the entire path. Sometimes we're asked to walk forward with nothing but blind faith. When we do, the universe meets us there—magnificently and sometimes miraculously.

I've carried this lesson with me ever since. It was a powerful reminder that when we hold the vision, stay in alignment, and take bold steps forward, the Universe handles the rest.

Another example is how I met my husband, Denis. I invested the time visualizing and feeling the emotions of being in a loving, joyful relationship with my soulmate. I didn't know how or when he would come into my life, but I trusted that the Universe was working behind the scenes. And it did. Our meeting happened in the most serendipitous way, and today we share a beautiful marriage filled with love and gratitude.

One of the most magical aspects of the Universe is how it brings your desires into form. Often the manifestations occur in ways that surprise and delight you—ways you could never have planned or predicted.

For instance, when I set the goal to become a *New York Times* best-selling author, I had no idea how it would happen. But I stayed aligned, visualized the outcome, and trusted the process. The Universe brought the right people, opportunities, and circumstances into my life to make it happen.

The Universe doesn't work on our timeline; it works on divine timing. It knows the perfect moment for everything to unfold, and it orchestrates events with precision and grace. Our role is to trust and allow, knowing that the Universe always has our back.

The most powerful state you can be in is one of relaxation and trust. When you relax in the knowing that your desire is already yours, you create a powerful magnetic pull that draws it into your life.

Relax in the knowing that the Universe is always working for your highest good.

Relax in the knowing that your desires are already manifested in the fourth dimension.

Relax in the knowing that the path to your manifestation is unfolding perfectly.

Relax in knowing that you can truly have anything you desire.

This state of trust and relaxation is not passive. It's an active choice to align with your desire and let go of resistance. When you relax in the knowing, you allow the Universe to do its work without interference.

I've witnessed countless examples of the Universe's magic in my own life and in the lives of others. One of my clients was struggling to grow her business and felt stuck in a cycle of fear and doubt. I encouraged her to align with her vision, trust the process, and relax in the knowing that her success was already hers.

Within months, opportunities began to flow to her effortlessly. She attracted high-paying clients, expanded her business, and achieved the financial freedom she had been dreaming of. The Universe responded to her alignment with miraculous precision.

The Universe is the most miraculous, incredible partner anyone could have. It doesn't require perfection; it simply requires alignment, trust, and faith. When you team up with the Universe, you unlock a power far greater than anything you could achieve on your own.

This partnership is available to you right now. It's always been there, waiting for you to plug in and connect. Are you ready to trust, align, and relax in the knowing that your desires are already yours?

The Universe has your back. Always.

11

Manifesting with Positive Prayer

How do most people pray? Often it's on their knees, with an energy of begging, hoping, or wishing. But here's the truth: prayer is energy directed into the Universe, and when we pour our energy into the problem, we often amplify it rather than resolve it. In this chapter, I want to guide you toward a more powerful, uplifting, and transformational way to pray—one that accelerates manifestation and deepens your connection with the divine.

I deeply value prayer, but my approach is different from many traditional methods. I practice prayers of thanks: prayers of gratitude for the blessings already present in my life, and for the things I desire, as if they have already manifested. Whether you are giving thanks for what is or what you wish to experience, the energy of gratitude shifts everything.

Consider this common prayer: "Oh, God, please bring me the money to pay my bills." Although sincere, this prayer reinforces lack. The focus is on the problem: unpaid bills. The Universe responds to the energy you send out, amplifying what you hold in your awareness. In essence, the prayer inadvertently magnifies financial struggle.

Now let's reshape that: "Thank you, God, for the abundant wealth that flows into my life. I am grateful that all of my financial needs are met with ease."

Feel the shift? One pleads for rescue; the other radiates confidence in the solution's existence. Positive prayer directs energy toward desired outcomes, not obstacles.

I invite you to cultivate a daily practice of positive prayer. Not just at night or before meals, but throughout the day, as a conscious alignment with gratitude and creation. Thank the Universe in advance for the life you are building, for the success already in your life, for the healing already done. This subtle yet profound shift magnetizes solutions and synchronizes your energy with your highest path.

Remember this: The Universe doesn't discriminate between what is real and what you imagine. It simply responds to the vibration you emit. Positive prayer lifts your frequency to match the reality you wish to create.

MY PERSONAL JOURNEY WITH POSITIVE PRAYER

When I faced health challenges, I didn't pray for healing by focusing on illness. I repeatedly gave thanks for my healthy, vibrant body. Even when I felt weak, I affirmed the strength within me. This wasn't about denial; it was about alignment. Over time, my body responded to the energy of gratitude and belief.

Positive prayer is not just for times of crisis. It can elevate your daily life, creating a foundation of peace, joy, and clarity. Every day,

I offer thanks for my family's love, health, and happiness. This isn't about fixing something broken; it's about amplifying what is beautiful and whole.

What can you pray for? Anything and everything. Positive prayer is rooted in appreciation and the expectation of good. It aligns perfectly with the transformative power of gratitude, making it accessible to everyone.

Try this tonight: Before you sleep, offer a prayer of thanks for the desires in your heart, imagining them as already fulfilled. Let the energy of joy and gratitude flood your being.

Examples of Positive Prayer in Action

"Thank you for the perfect opportunities that are in my life."
"I am so grateful for the love and harmony in my relationships."
"Thank you for my radiant health and boundless energy."
"I give thanks for the financial prosperity that flows to me with ease."
"I am grateful for the peace and clarity that surrounds me."

Positive prayer isn't just about manifesting material things. It can transform the way you experience the world. Begin small, offering prayers of thanks for simple joys: a sunny day, a kind word, a peaceful moment. The more you engage in this practice, the more natural it becomes. Soon positive prayer will feel like second nature, an ongoing dialogue of gratitude and creation with the Universe.

Manifestation begins the moment you shift from asking to thanking.

You are the architect of your reality, and positive prayer is one of the most powerful tools at your disposal. Embrace it fully and watch as your world transforms.

12

The Ripple Effect of Choice

YEARS AGO, A WOMAN came to me for guidance. She became one of my high-end private mentoring clients. Although she initially sought my help to grow her career, during one of our early sessions, she revealed a deep sense of failure—not in her business, but in her personal life.

She confided that she had married a man she knew wasn't right for her. Even as he proposed, she felt inner resistance. But the allure of being engaged, planning a wedding, and stepping into the role of a wife overshadowed her intuition. She didn't love him; she loved the *idea* of the experience.

On her wedding day, with every step down the aisle, her heart whispered, "Turn back," yet she continued forward. When the time came, she said "I do" while every fiber of her being silently screamed, "Run."

For years, she convinced herself that she could grow to love him. The lifestyle he offered was appealing, and she held on to the hope that perhaps love would blossom. But it never did.

When I asked if she desired something different—something more aligned with her heart—she hesitated. She had long given up, convinced it was too late. She believed that the path she had chosen led to a dead end, and there was no turning back.

I gently reminded her of a profound truth: *the greatest gift we've been given is the gift of choice.* No matter how far down a road we've traveled, we can always choose a different path.

I could see the spark of possibility ignite in her eyes as she imagined an alternate life—a life filled with love, passion, and fulfillment. That spark grew into action.

Shortly after, she had an honest, vulnerable conversation with her husband. To her surprise, he too had been quietly unhappy. He confessed that while he had feelings for a coworker, he had remained faithful to their vows. They respected each other, but their relationship had settled into a comfortable, sibling-like bond.

Their conversation led to a mutual decision to part ways—not out of anger or regret, but with kindness and understanding. They divorced and maintained a loving friendship. In time, both found their soulmates and built the lives they once only imagined. Today they even socialize as couples, bonded by a shared past and mutual respect.

This story, while not tragic, carried one lingering sadness: they had both longed for children but had waited. By the time they separated, the window of opportunity had passed.

Could a different decision early on have led to a different outcome? Undoubtedly. But the past cannot be rewritten.

What *can* be shaped is the present—and the future.

Every decision we make sends ripples into the world. For every action, there is an equal reaction. This is not just a scientific principle; it is a universal law that governs every aspect of our lives.

Consider this: reading this book was a decision. The insights you gain—and the actions you take as a result—will ripple into your future. You are already in the process of activating change.

Reflecting on my own life, I see how pivotal decisions shaped my path. Choosing to study in 1979, committing to self-discipline, and dedicating myself to serving others all set in motion a chain of events that led me to the success and joy I now experience.

Some decisions reveal their effects almost immediately. Others, like seeds planted in fertile soil, take time to bloom. But make no mistake—*every* decision holds power.

Your life is not the sum of random events. It is the outcome of choices—some deliberate, some unconscious, but all significant.

Right now, you stand at the edge of possibility. Every choice you make from this moment forward shapes the future you will experience.

If the past has taught you anything, let it be this: *the next step is always within your control.*

You don't need to wait for the "perfect" moment. You don't need to map out every detail of the journey. All you need is the courage to choose again—and the willingness to trust that your next decision is creating ripples that will guide you toward the life you desire.

So take that step. Let the ripple begin.

Part II
Unblocking the Path to Creation

13

The Truth That Sets You Free

As you move into this next section of the book, I invite you to approach it with curiosity, enthusiasm, and above all, self-compassion. This is not about judgment or self-criticism: it's about uncovering the truths that might be holding you back from the life you deserve. It's about learning how to shift from unconscious resistance to conscious alignment with your desires.

The Universe isn't withholding anything from you. If your desires haven't manifested, it's not because you're not good enough or because the Universe isn't on your side. It's because, on some level, you've been standing in your own way. This isn't about judgment—it's about awareness.

Manifestation requires alignment: alignment between your thoughts, feelings, beliefs, and the actions you take. When all of these are in harmony, you are unstoppable. But when there's a block—whether it's doubt, fear, unworthiness, or impatience—it's like throwing a wrench into the gears of creation. The flow of energy slows down, and progress feels stalled.

Here's the good news: these blocks are not permanent. They're simply patterns, habits, and beliefs that have been running in the background of your mind. Once you determine what they are and no longer give them any thought or continue to emotionalize them, they lose their power. You have the ability to transform these blocks into stepping stones that lead you directly to your desires.

If you're wondering who might be holding you back, take a look in the mirror. And if you're wondering who has the power to help you achieve everything you desire, look in the mirror again.

This truth might feel uncomfortable at first, but it's also incredibly freeing. Why? Because if you are the one holding yourself back, that means you also have the power to move yourself forward. You are not at the mercy of circumstances, other people, or even your past. You are the creator of your reality, and the power to create is always within you, and the moment to create is right now, this very moment.

I know this because I've experienced it firsthand. After my divorce, I was carrying a deep belief that I wasn't worthy of love. I didn't even realize it at the time, but that belief was shaping my reality. It was a block that kept me from attracting the kind of relationship I truly desired. If I hadn't done the inner work to change that belief, I would have never met and married my soulmate, Denis.

The same is true for a client of mine who came to me feeling deeply unworthy of success. She was caught in a cycle of self-doubt, constantly questioning whether she deserved the kind of life she dreamed of. If she had held on to that belief, she would have never experienced the incredible success she enjoys today—success that continues to grow year after year.

Power is always available to you. It's not something outside of you; it's something within. But if you're not accessing that power, or if you're unknowingly doing things that are in direct opposition to your desires, it's like trying to drive a car with the emergency brake on. The car might still move, but it's going to take a lot more effort and strain.

Recognizing these blocks is not about judging yourself; it's about liberating yourself. When you approach this next section with an open mind and a willingness to take an honest look at your patterns, you'll be giving yourself the greatest gift: the freedom to create a life that truly excites and fulfills you.

Here's the best part: while recognizing and removing blocks is essential, it's only the beginning. The real magic happens when you fully embrace the practical application of being in the *moment of creation*—when you live aligned with your desires as your dominant way of being.

This is where the transformation becomes undeniable, where the results start to flow with ease, and where life seems filled with miracles. The last section of this book will be your icing on the cake. It will take everything you've learned and show you how to live in a way that amplifies your ability to create a life that feels truly magical. Great materials are coming your way: tools, techniques, and practices that will empower you to align, stay aligned, and thrive.

As you move forward, I encourage you to embrace this process with enthusiasm. These blocks aren't here to stop you; they're here to teach you. They're showing you where your alignment is off so that you can course-correct and get back on track.

As you explore the specific blocks in the chapters ahead, remember: no matter how ingrained a block may feel, it's never permanent. You have the power to change it. You have the power to rise above it. And you have the power to create a life that exceeds even your wildest dreams.

The path to unblocking your flow begins now.

14

Understanding the Three Levels of Resistance

IN THE PROCESS OF creation, few things are as frustrating as feeling stuck. You set an intention, visualize the outcome, and even take steps forward, yet something feels off. It's as if an invisible wall rises between you and your desire. That wall isn't external. It resides within, and it shows up as blocks. But not all blocks are the same.

To dismantle what holds you back, it's essential to understand the nature of the block you're facing. There are three primary types of blocks:

1. Surface blocks
2. Intermediate blocks
3. Core (deep) blocks

Each level of resistance operates differently, and the approach to dissolving them varies. Let's explore each one.

SURFACE BLOCKS: EVERYDAY RESISTANCE

Surface blocks are the most common and easiest to recognize. They show up as procrastination, minor doubts, or excuses that feel almost habitual. You might experience them as a reluctance to take action, hesitation when opportunities arise, or a lingering voice that questions whether you're ready.

These blocks often stem from temporary states of mind. They can be triggered by a lack of focus, external distractions, or fatigue. Surface blocks are like clouds passing through a clear sky: they obscure your vision briefly but are relatively easy to shift.

Examples of surface blocks:
- "I'll start tomorrow."
- "I'm not sure if I have the time right now."
- "Maybe I should wait until I feel more confident."

Scenario: Sandy wanted to start painting as a hobby but found herself consistently putting it off. She told herself she didn't have the right supplies, the lighting in her home wasn't good enough, and she would start "next weekend." One evening, she decided to break the pattern by simply picking up a pencil and sketching for ten minutes. That small action dissolved the block, and she quickly rediscovered her passion for art.

How to Dissolve Surface Blocks
- Shift your environment.
- Take one small step immediately.
- Remind yourself that perfection isn't necessary to begin.

INTERMEDIATE BLOCKS: PATTERNS AND BELIEFS

Intermediate blocks dig deeper into your subconscious. These blocks are shaped by patterns developed over time—habitual thought loops, limiting beliefs, and conditioned responses. Unlike surface blocks, intermediate blocks persist even after motivation kicks in. They often manifest as recurring fears or self-sabotaging behaviors that prevent long-term progress. Addressing intermediate blocks requires identifying the pattern and interrupting it consciously.

Examples of intermediate blocks:
- "I've never been good at this, so why try?"
- "Success means more responsibility, and I'm not ready for that."
- "Whenever I start to make progress, something goes wrong."

Scenario: James had a habit of avoiding leadership opportunities at work. Each time he was offered a promotion, he declined, telling himself that more responsibility would lead to burnout. After reflecting, he realized this belief stemmed from watching his father work long hours, rarely spending time with the family. By rewriting his belief—"leadership will bring balance and fulfillment"—James accepted his next promotion and thrived in his new role.

How to Dissolve Intermediate Blocks
- Journaling to uncover recurring patterns
- Affirmations and rewiring beliefs through repetition
- Consistent small wins to prove old beliefs wrong

CORE (DEEP) BLOCKS: THE ROOT OF RESISTANCE

Core blocks lie at the foundation of who you are. They are deeply ingrained and often linked to formative experiences, childhood conditioning, or past traumas. These blocks shape your identity, often limiting what you believe is possible for your life.

Core blocks can manifest as an overarching feeling of unworthiness, fear of abandonment, or a deep mistrust in the flow of life. Dissolving them requires inner work, self-reflection, and often guidance from mentors, coaches, or spiritual practices.

Examples of core blocks:
- "I'm not deserving of happiness or success."
- "If I pursue this dream, I might lose relationships."
- "Failure defines who I am."

Scenario: Emily had dreamed of writing a book since childhood, but she never started. Deep down, she believed her voice didn't matter. This belief stemmed from years of being told to stay quiet and not express herself. Through deep self-work, affirmations, and my support as her mentor, Emily began writing small articles and blog posts. Eventually, she overcame the core belief and published her first book, inspiring others to share their stories.

How to Dissolve Core Blocks
- Inner child healing and forgiveness work
- Meditation and visualization practices
- Working with a coach, therapist, or mentor to uncover root causes

RECOGNIZING AND RESPECTING THE PROCESS

Blocks are not signs of failure. They are part of the human experience. Each block you face is an opportunity to grow, recalibrate, and align more deeply with your desires.

Understanding whether you're dealing with surface, intermediate, or core blocks allows you to approach the path of creation with greater clarity. By addressing these blocks at their respective levels, you remove the resistance and allow the flow of your desires to manifest more effortlessly.

In the following chapters, we will dive deeper into each type of block, exploring how they arise and how you can work through them effectively.

For now, simply ask yourself: *where am I feeling stuck, and what type of block might I be facing?* The answer to that question holds the key to your next breakthrough.

15

Recognizing the Blocks on Your Path

KNOWLEDGE IS A POWERFUL tool. Sometimes the simple act of recognizing what holds you back can spark the transformation you've been seeking. In the next part, we'll explore the various stages where blocks arise and how they silently shape the course of your life.

Blocks aren't always obvious. Some sit quietly beneath the surface, influencing decisions without us even realizing it. Others are more pronounced, showing up as procrastination, fear, or self-doubt. Whether subtle or glaring, these blocks can keep you from reaching your fullest potential.

As you read through the following examples, allow yourself to reflect. Pay attention to any descriptions that resonate. Perhaps you'll recognize a thought pattern, habit, or emotion that mirrors your own experience. This isn't a coincidence: it's an opportunity for awareness.

By the end of this section, you may find yourself thinking, "Oh, that's me!" or "I've been there before." That moment of recognition is key, because once you see the block, you can begin to clear it.

This part of the book is about illumination. The final sections will focus on practical application and treatment, guiding you step by step toward dissolving these blocks and aligning fully with your desires.

Let's have fun with this.

16

The Twelve Blocks Standing between You and Success

AWARENESS IS THE FIRST step to freedom. Once you see the block, you hold the power to dissolve it.

1. THE PRE-GOAL BLOCK: LIMITING BELIEFS

Long before a goal even takes shape, something quieter but equally powerful begins to stir—limiting beliefs. These are the whispered doubts that echo through your mind, the subtle yet persistent voice that convinces you not to reach too far. They're born from experiences tucked away in the past, woven together by societal conditioning or the well-meaning but restrictive messages we absorbed in childhood. Without realizing it, these beliefs create a boundary around what feels possible.

The moment a spark of desire appears, the mind counters with hesitation:

"Who am I to think I can do this?"

"People like me don't achieve things like that."

"I'm too old. If it hasn't happened by now, it never will."

These thoughts aren't loud or aggressive. They slip in gently, almost like background noise, but their impact is profound. They clip the wings of potential before it even has the chance to take flight. You might find yourself dreaming smaller, rationalizing why something isn't worth the risk, or settling for less because reaching higher feels too vulnerable.

I've seen this effect countless times in clients I've worked with—people who arrived with beautiful visions for their lives but who couldn't shake the weight of past failures or deep-seated insecurities. One client in particular, Dana, embodied this block perfectly.

Dana was in her late sixties when she first came to me, expressing a desire to write a book. She wanted to leave something meaningful behind, a legacy that would outlive her. But each time she considered sitting down to write, doubt clouded her vision.

"What's the point?" she told me. "Who wants to read about what I have to say? Maybe I've waited too long."

Her words weren't unique. I had heard variations of that same sentence from people of all ages. But here's the thing—Dana's belief wasn't based on reality. It was simply a story she had told herself over the years, and the more she repeated it, the more real it seemed.

I asked Dana to take a moment to remember a time in her life when she accomplished something she once thought impossible. After some reflection, she recalled how, years ago, she managed to transition into a new career later in life, a feat she once considered beyond her reach.

"See?" I told her. "That wasn't too late. Why should this be any different?"

Little by little, Dana began challenging her own narrative. She started writing, not with the goal of publishing right away, but just to get the words flowing. With each page she completed, the limiting beliefs weakened. Eventually, she finished her book—one that resonated deeply with readers, who found inspiration in her journey.

Limiting beliefs thrive in silence. They grow stronger when left unchecked, shaping the reality you experience. But the moment you question them, they begin to crumble.

If you ever find yourself hesitating, remember Dana. Reflect on the quiet victories you've already had. The goal isn't to overpower doubt in a single day but to take small steps forward despite it. Every action you take chips away at those invisible walls, until suddenly you realize the only thing keeping you from moving forward was the belief that you couldn't.

Overcoming the Block

The first step is awareness—recognizing these limiting thoughts as the stories they are, not absolute truths. From there, start small:

- Recall past wins, no matter how minor they seem.
- Immerse yourself in the stories of others who overcame similar doubts.
- Use affirmations, but don't just repeat them—*feel* them.

Visualize yourself achieving that goal, as if the outcome is inevitable.

When you dare to stretch beyond the boundaries of limiting beliefs, you step into the realm of possibility—and that's where the real magic happens.

2. THE DREAMING STAGE BLOCK: FEAR OF FAILURE

You've finally dared to let your mind wander toward the possibilities—the kind of life you could live, the goals you could achieve. But just as that vision begins to take shape, a shadow creeps in, whispering louder than the dream itself: *what if I fail?* The thought plants itself firmly, almost like an uninvited guest who refuses to leave.

The fear doesn't just hover in the background; it makes itself comfortable. You imagine scenarios where things unravel: public embarrassment, quiet judgment from friends and family, the sinking feeling of disappointing yourself.

You might find yourself caught in the endless loop of planning without moving forward. The dream feels safer when it's confined to your imagination, untouched by the risk of reality. After all, as long as you don't try, you can't fail.

Common thoughts:

"What if I fail?"

"People will judge me if I don't succeed."

"I don't want to disappoint myself or others."

The weight of this fear often keeps dreams locked away, like fragile glass behind cabinet doors. It feels easier to leave them untouched than risk breaking them.

But here's the truth: failure is inevitable. It's not a curse or a sign to stop; it's a breadcrumb on the path to success. Every person who has built something extraordinary can point to moments where they stumbled, redirected, and tried again.

One of my clients once shared her fear of launching a business after years of working in a secure corporate role. She envisioned the ridicule if things didn't pan out, even picturing former colleagues gossiping. But after months of hesitation, she took one small step—testing her idea with a small group. That single action sparked a series of breakthroughs. Although she faced hurdles, she quickly learned that failure was far less catastrophic than she had imagined.

Overcoming the Block

- Reframing failure as feedback transforms how you interact with it. Rather than seeing it as an ending, view it as a stepping stone that refines and clarifies your path. Each misstep carries lessons that prepare you for the next stage.
- Begin by shrinking the scale. Take small actions that allow you to experience low-risk failure and build resilience. Test ideas in safe environments.
- Gather insights and keep moving forward. Fear loses its grip the moment you start moving. Action—no matter how small—is the antidote to doubt.

3. GOAL-SETTING BLOCK: LACK OF CLARITY

You sit down, ready to craft the next chapter of your life. The excitement flickers, but almost immediately, the overwhelm sets in. Where do I even begin? The mind feels cluttered with ideas that tug you in different directions. Each path seems appealing, but none stands out as the one.

For some, the challenge isn't a lack of ideas: it's too many. The brain floods with possibilities, leaving you paralyzed by the fear of choosing the wrong path. For others, the opposite holds true: there's a fog where inspiration should be. The desire for change is there, but the destination remains blurry.

Common thoughts:

"I'm not sure what I really want."

"I have too many ideas and can't pick one."

"What if I choose the wrong path?"

The result? Indecision becomes the default. Rather than take a step, you stay still—hoping for a lightning bolt of clarity, which rarely arrives on its own.

A client once told me, "I know I'm meant to do something, but I don't know what that is." She'd been circling the same ideas for years, dabbling in different projects but never committing fully. After months of inertia, I encouraged her to pick one small idea—not forever, just for now. It was like planting a single seed in the vast garden of her imagination. That small action created momentum, and over time, the clarity she craved started to unfold naturally.

Overcoming the Block

Clarity often doesn't arrive in one grand epiphany. It reveals itself through movement—like a road that curves, showing more of the landscape the further you travel.

- Give yourself permission to explore.
- Test ideas, take imperfect action, and let the experience shape your next step.
- Break large, intimidating goals into smaller, digestible parts. Sometimes the vision forms not in the stillness, but in the doing.

Even if the first step isn't exactly right, it will lead you closer to what feels aligned. The worst thing you can do is wait for certainty before beginning.

4. THE DESIRE BLOCK: STAYING IN A STATE OF WANTING

Desire is a powerful force. It stirs the imagination, paints vivid pictures of what life could look like, and ignites a spark of hope. But for many, desire becomes a comfortable space—one they linger in for years without ever stepping forward. The line between wishing and doing can feel deceptively thin, yet it often separates those who achieve their dreams from those who don't.

I once worked with a client named Julia, who had spent years dreaming of becoming a published author. Every time we spoke, she would light up with excitement as she described her ideas for a novel. Yet each conversation ended the same way. "One day," she'd say. "I just need to find the right time."

That right time never seemed to come. Julia's desire remained a distant star she admired but never tried to reach. Months passed, then years, and the story she longed to write lived only in her mind.

The problem wasn't Julia's lack of talent or passion. It was her comfort in wanting. Desire, when left unchecked, creates the illusion of movement without actual progress. Like watering seeds but never planting them, you nurture the dream but never give it the soil it needs to grow.

One day, after yet another call where Julia described her unwritten book, I said, "Julia, what if you just write one page this week? Not the whole thing. Just one."

She hesitated but agreed. The next time we spoke, she had written three pages. That small action broke the cycle. Julia began shifting from someone who wants to write to someone who writes.

When desire isn't met with action, dreams stay dreams. The longer you remain in the state of wanting, the more comfortable it becomes to believe the fantasy is enough.

Common thoughts:

"I wish I could have that."

"One day I'll make it happen."

"It would be nice if . . ."

Overcoming the Block

The shift happens the moment you make a clear decision.

- Stop waiting for perfect conditions or the elusive "right time."
- Begin where you are. Decide today to take one tangible step forward, no matter how small.
- Desire will always be part of the journey, but the real transformation comes when you move from wishing to doing.

Julia eventually finished her novel, but she later admitted that the hardest part wasn't writing—it was deciding to start.

The difference between longing for something and living it is often just one decision away.

5. THE ACTION BLOCK: PROCRASTINATION AND PERFECTIONISM

Even with a crystal clear goal, taking the first step can feel like scaling a mountain. The mind races ahead, crafting scenarios of failure, embarrassment, or worse—imperfection. Procrastination and perfectionism creep in, often disguised as noble qualities like thorough preparation or waiting for the right time.

I once worked with a medical doctor who had spent over two decades building a successful career. Despite her accomplishments, she felt a persistent tug toward something else—starting her own wellness practice, which would allow her to help patients in a more holistic way.

She was brilliant, driven, and deeply passionate. But there was one thing that consistently stood in her way—perfectionism. Every time she began planning her new business, she convinced herself she wasn't ready.

"I need to complete more courses," she'd say. "I can't launch this until every detail is flawless. What if I make a mistake?"

Her medical training had conditioned her to avoid errors at all costs, and that mindset bled into her entrepreneurial ambitions. Whereas perfection had served her in the operating room, it was paralyzing her in the world of business.

Perfectionism often masquerades as preparation. This lady doctor had notebooks filled with plans, spreadsheets detailing potential expenses, and vision boards stacked with ideas. But none of it translated into action.

One day during our session, I asked her, "Hey, what if you gave yourself permission to start messy? What if you helped just one person, without needing everything to be perfect?"

She hesitated but agreed to try. Instead of waiting until every component of her practice was in place, she started small, offering weekend wellness workshops from her home. The first session wasn't flawless, but it was real. That realness fueled her confidence to take the next step.

Waiting for perfection leads to endless delay. While you may feel you're making progress by "getting ready," it's often just a comfortable form of procrastination.

Common thoughts:
"I'll start tomorrow."
"I need to be fully prepared first."
"It's not the right time yet."

Overcoming the Block

The antidote to perfectionism is progress.
- Start small.
- Start messy.
- Start with one action that inches you closer to your goal. Every imperfect step builds momentum, and momentum is far more powerful than waiting for the elusive "perfect moment."

My client's wellness business is now thriving. She later admitted that if she had waited for everything to align, she might never have started. Her success didn't come from perfect preparation: it came from the courage to begin.

The first step doesn't need to be grand. It just needs to be taken.

6. THE PROGRESS BLOCK: SELF-SABOTAGE

Sometimes the biggest obstacle isn't at the starting line; it's just as you're gaining momentum. Progress feels exciting, but for some, it triggers an unsettling sense of discomfort. This is the realm of self-sabotage. It's often subtle, driven by hidden fears or a lingering sense of unworthiness. Just as things begin to align, the mind throws up reasons to pause or retreat.

I remember working with a client named Igor, a talented entrepreneur who had finally hit his stride. After years of struggling to launch his business, he landed a major client contract that would open doors to even more opportunities. He was thrilled, but within days, his demeanor shifted. He started rescheduling meetings, missing deadlines, and doubting whether he could handle the workload.

When I asked him about it, he admitted, "I feel like maybe I'm not ready. This happened too fast . . . what if I mess it all up?"

Igor's fear wasn't unusual. Success can feel foreign, especially if you've spent years fighting for it. Sometimes achieving progress feels riskier than staying in struggle, because the higher the climb, the further the fall.

Self-sabotage can sneak in quietly, unraveling progress in the most frustrating ways. You might procrastinate, pick fights with loved ones, or "accidentally" miss out on opportunities. Without recognizing this pattern, long-term success becomes difficult to sustain.

Igor didn't see it at first, but as we unpacked his fears, he realized he'd always pulled back when things started to go well. It was an unconscious defense mechanism to avoid disappointment.

I asked Igor to visualize himself already succeeding. We reinforced the idea that he was worthy of the opportunities coming his way. He began practicing daily affirmations like, "I deserve success, and I allow it to stay." Little by little, he leaned into progress instead of away from it.

Within six months, Igor's business had tripled in growth. The moment he realized he wasn't standing in his own way was the moment he unlocked a new level of confidence and prosperity.

Common thoughts:

"Maybe I'm not ready."

"This is too good to be true."

"I always ruin things when they go well."

Overcoming the Block

The first step in disarming self-sabotage is awareness. Recognize the pattern early. When things start flowing, pay attention to the subtle ways you might resist or downplay success. Then meet yourself with compassion.

Self-sabotage may visit, but it doesn't have to stay. Growth is not a fluke. It's a reflection of the energy you consistently embody.

7. THE PLATEAU BLOCK: FEAR OF SUCCESS

While fear of failure often gets the spotlight, there's a quieter but equally powerful force that can stall progress: fear of success. This block is deceptive because on the surface, success seems like the ultimate goal. Yet beneath the excitement lies an undercurrent of doubt. What if success changes your life too much, brings new pressures, or raises expectations you don't feel ready for?

I once worked with a client named Abagail, a brilliant graphic designer who had built a thriving freelance business. Her work was exceptional, and she had all the skills needed to scale her business to new heights. But whenever opportunities to expand came her way—like partnering with larger companies or hiring a team—she hesitated.

One day she admitted, "I know I could grow, but what if I can't keep up? I'd rather stay small than risk burning out or disappointing clients."

Abagail wasn't afraid of failing; she was afraid of what succeeding might demand of her. She feared the responsibility that came with growth. In her mind, success wasn't just more income or recognition. It was more work, more visibility, and more pressure to stay at the top.

Fear of success can create invisible ceilings. You might stop pursuing new opportunities or downplay your skills to avoid standing out. It's a protective mechanism, but one that keeps you small.

Abagail found herself in this exact place. Every time she reached a certain income level, she unconsciously slowed down her marketing or declined new projects, staying within the comfort zone she knew she could manage.

Common thoughts:

"Can I really handle success?"

"What if I lose it all?"

"Success will mean more pressure and expectations."

Overcoming the Block

The first step in overcoming the fear of success is to redefine what success looks like. Success doesn't have to mean overwhelm or exhaustion. I guided Abagail to visualize success as expansion—a life of ease, abundance, and balance. Instead of picturing a chaotic future, we painted a vision of her thriving, delegating tasks, and enjoying the rewards of her hard work.

She began adopting the belief that success doesn't complicate life; it can simplify it. Abagail eventually hired an assistant, outsourced parts of her workload, and embraced growth. Within a year, her income doubled, and she was working less, not more.

Fear of success isn't about whether you're capable—it's about trusting that you can handle the expansion gracefully. And the truth is, you can.

8. THE COMMITMENT BLOCK: LACK OF PERSISTENCE

Starting something new is exciting. The initial rush of setting a goal and envisioning the results can light a fire within. But what happens when the novelty wears off and progress feels slower than expected? This is where many people falter—not because they lack ability, but because they mistake slow progress for no progress.

I once worked with someone who had a clear vision of creating an online coaching business. In the first few months, they were unstoppable—building a website, crafting offers, and eagerly promoting their services. But after a few launches that didn't yield the results they hoped for, doubt crept in.

"I'm doing everything right," they said. "But it's not happening fast enough. Maybe I'm not cut out for this."

They were convinced that because the breakthrough hadn't arrived yet, it never would. They didn't realize that they were much closer than they thought.

Lack of persistence often leads to abandoned dreams right on the cusp of success. Progress can be slow, but without consistent effort, goals slip through the cracks just before they materialize.

Common thoughts:

"This is taking too long."

"Maybe this isn't meant for me."

"I don't see results, so why keep going?"

Overcoming the Block

Persistence isn't about sprinting to the finish line; it's about showing up daily, even when results aren't immediately visible. In this case, I encouraged my client to shift their focus to small wins—the emails they received, the followers that steadily grew, the connections that deepened.

We celebrated every milestone, no matter how small, and I reminded them of one truth: the Universe rewards consistency. Eventually their breakthrough came—not in a single, dramatic moment but as a culmination of steady, persistent action. By staying the course, they turned a struggling side hustle into a full-time business.

9. THE MINDSET BLOCK: NEGATIVE SELF-TALK

Sometimes the loudest critic we face isn't external—it's the voice inside our own head. Negative self-talk can be subtle, like a faint whisper of doubt, or deafening, drowning out any possibility of success. It's the constant hum of "I'm not enough" or "I'll never figure this out."

I once worked with a woman whom I'll call Sarah, who, like many of the clients I have been blessed to serve, had been dreaming of writing her first book. Every time she sat down to start, a voice in her head told her, "Who are you to write a book? You're not an author. No one will care what you have to say."

Sarah confided that this wasn't the first time she'd heard that voice. It echoed comments from a childhood teacher who once told her she lacked creativity. Even decades later, the words had planted roots deep in her mind. I personally had the same thoughts echo in my mind before I wrote my first book.

Negative self-talk acts like an invisible chain, holding you back from even taking the first step. Over time, it erodes confidence and reinforces a sense of inadequacy, making progress feel impossible.

Common thoughts:

"I'm not cut out for this."
"Others are better than me."
"I'll never be able to do this."

Overcoming the Block

I encouraged Sarah to try a simple exercise: each time the negative voice appeared, she would pause and respond with kindness, as if speaking to her best friend. When she heard "I'm not good enough," she replaced it with "I have a story worth telling, and my voice matters."

We also incorporated affirmations and daily visualization practices. Sarah began to see herself as a successful author, feeling the joy of holding her finished book. Slowly the negative self-talk lost its grip.

Months later, Sarah not only finished her book but published it, receiving heartfelt messages from readers who were inspired by her words.

Negative self-talk may not disappear overnight, but with consistent effort, it can transform into one of your greatest strengths—a voice that cheers you on rather than holds you back.

10. THE RESULTS BLOCK: IMPATIENCE AND DOUBT

Impatience often sneaks in when you've been diligently working toward a goal, but the results seem hidden beneath the surface. It's like planting seeds and standing over the soil, wondering why nothing is sprouting after a few days. The longer the wait, the louder doubt becomes, whispering that maybe the effort isn't worth it.

I remember working with a client, Chris, who had set his sights on transforming his finances. After months of applying affirmations, visualization, and consistent action, he saw no significant shifts. Despite his best efforts, his financial situation remained unchanged—or so it seemed.

Chris called me one afternoon and said, "Peggy, I've been doing everything right, but nothing's happening. Maybe I'm never going to be wealthy." I could hear the frustration in his voice.

Impatience often leads to self-sabotage or abandoning the process altogether. People walk away just before their breakthrough, unaware that results were already in motion.

Common thoughts:

"Why isn't this working?"

"I'm putting in effort, but nothing's happening."

"Maybe I'm wasting my time."

Overcoming the Block

I reminded Chris that unseen progress is still progress. I shared how bamboo spends years developing roots underground before breaking through the soil—and when it does, it grows rapidly. I encouraged him to continue trusting the process, even if he couldn't see immediate evidence.

A few weeks later, Chris received a surprising opportunity—an unexpected offer that significantly increased his income. He told me, "I almost gave up, but I kept going because of that conversation. Now I realize things were shifting all along."

The key to overcoming impatience is to focus on faith over frustration. Trust that every small step counts, even when you can't see the full picture yet.

11. THE AIMLESS BLOCK: FEELING LOST

There's a unique kind of frustration that comes from feeling directionless. It's as if you're standing at a crossroads with no signs, unsure of which path to take. This uncertainty can create hesitation, leaving dreams unexplored and potential unrealized.

Pisey, a client of mine, knew this feeling all too well. English wasn't her first language, though she could speak and read it fluently. Deep down, she had a desire to share her story by writing a book—but every time she tried, she felt paralyzed. Pisey would write a few pages, read them over, and then promptly discard them.

"I just don't think I can do this," she admitted during one of our sessions. She felt overwhelmed by self-doubt, convinced that the process of writing was too big of a leap for someone like her.

Pisey's fear of not being good enough caused her to repeatedly abandon the project, keeping her stuck in a cycle of false starts and self-criticism. Like many others, she mistook feeling lost for a lack of ability.

Common thoughts:

"I don't know what I really want."

"There are too many choices, and I can't decide."

"I feel stuck and unsure where to start."

Overcoming the Block

I encouraged Pisey to let go of the need for perfection and just start somewhere. I assured her that clarity often comes through action, not from waiting for the "perfect" plan to reveal itself. With some gentle guidance, Pisey agreed to tackle the book one section at a time, allowing the process to unfold naturally.

As the pages accumulated, Pisey's confidence grew. She stopped throwing away drafts and began seeing her story take shape. Eventually, not only did she complete the book but she published it—and it became an international best seller.

Pisey's journey is a reminder that feeling lost isn't a permanent state. The path often becomes clearer while walking it.

Takeaway: If you feel aimless, allow yourself to experiment. Take small steps in multiple directions until the right one resonates. Progress doesn't require certainty; it only requires a willingness to begin.

12. THE RESPONSIBILITY BLOCK: BLAMING

Blame can be one of the most deceptive blocks to progress. It feels justified—pointing fingers at external circumstances or people who seem to have shaped our struggles. However, the moment we allow blame to take root, we unknowingly give away our power to create change.

I know this block well, because I lived it. In 1979, I was stuck in a cycle of blame that felt endless. I genuinely believed my life was miserable because of other people. If my parents had been different, if my boss hadn't been so dismissive, if circumstances had just been better, maybe I'd finally be happy.

It was easy to cast responsibility outward. After all, acknowledging my own role in the situation would have meant facing the uncomfortable truth that I wasn't doing much to change things.

Blame shackled me to my current situation and fueled resentment and helplessness. Every time I shifted responsibility away from myself, I felt less capable of improving my life. It was a trap, and it kept me stuck longer than I care to admit.

Common thoughts:

"It's their fault my life is a mess."

"If circumstances were different, I'd be further along."

"I can't change things because of others."

Overcoming the Block

The turning point came when I realized that no one was coming to save me. If I wanted a better life, I had to create it. I decided to stop blaming and start taking ownership, even when it felt unfair or uncomfortable.

I began by focusing on small areas where I did have control—changing my mindset, setting goals, and pursuing opportunities. Slowly but surely, this shift led to bigger changes. I left the job I hated, found work I loved, and began building a life that reflected my desires, not my excuses.

Taking responsibility didn't just alter my life; it empowered me to help others break free from the same block.

Takeaway: Blame may feel like protection, but it's really a prison. Reclaim your power by asking, "What will I do right now to move forward?" Even the smallest steps can shatter the illusion of helplessness and can open doors to transformation.

YOUR MOMENT OF POWER

As you reflect on the blocks discussed above, ask yourself whether any of them have resonated with you. If so, have you made a firm decision to move past or overcome them? This is your moment of power! Awareness is a game changer because it gives you clarity, and clarity means you can now see where to focus your energy. When you truly see, you unlock the potential to shift your reality.

Embrace the excitement of this awareness! The power to create a new path is in your hands. With this clarity, you can start to break free from the patterns that have held you back and begin aligning with your true potential. Remember, the moment of *now* is always available to you. With each choice you make today, you are stepping closer to manifesting your dreams.

In the next section, we'll explore powerful techniques and strategies to help you dissolve these blocks for good.

Part III

Action into Creation: The Tools for Transformation

17

The Second Wind

THERE ARE MOMENTS IN every journey when you feel you've reached the end of your rope, when your energy is spent, and you wonder if you can push through. It's in these moments that the most powerful victories are achieved—by choosing not to give up.

MARK TEWKSBURY AND THE POWER OF BELIEF

One of the most inspiring examples of perseverance comes from Canadian swimmer Mark Tewksbury, who faced his own moment of decision at the 1992 Summer Olympics in Barcelona. Tewksbury had already earned his place in Olympic history in 1988 by winning medals, but his heart was set on one thing: the gold medal in the hundred-meter backstroke.

In 1988, Mark had come close, but his dreams were not fully realized. He returned to the 1992 Olympics with a single mission: to claim the gold medal. At the time, Mark was not favored to win.

Many experts didn't believe he had what it would take to defeat the competition. But Mark had a secret weapon: a firm belief in the process of creation and the power of visualization.

He practiced the principles that we explore in this book: living in the *moment of creation*. He imagined himself already winning, feeling the rush of excitement as he saw his name listed as the gold medalist, hearing the crowd cheering for him, and savoring the joy of success.

The day before the competition, Mark went to the pool area and visualized the entire race. He imagined himself swimming, finishing first, and seeing his name on the board as the gold medal winner. He immersed himself fully in the feelings of already having won.

On the day of the competition, Mark arrived at the "ready room" and noticed that he didn't feel exactly ready. Doubt crept in, but he didn't let it consume him. Instead, he entered the spirit of the moment and refocused. He closed out everything else around him and visualized once again. When the race began, Mark could feel the pressure mounting. As the swimmers powered ahead, he saw an elbow move out of the corner of his eye, a signal that he was slightly behind.

Instead of panicking, Mark remained calm and continued to chant in his mind, "Go now." With every "Go now," he pushed himself harder, stronger, and faster, all while staying completely aligned with the vision he had created. His mind remained focused on victory, and as he touched the wall, he knew that he had done it. He had won.

Sure enough, when Mark came out of the water, he looked up to see his name in first place: *Mark Tewksbury, Gold*. His belief, visualization, and unwavering trust in the process had made it happen. It was the culmination of years of dedication, discipline, and faith, as well as the moment when the Universe responded to his commitment and vision.

DENIS AND THE MARATHON FINISH LINE

My husband, Denis, experienced his own moment of perseverance during his first half marathon. He loved running, and the exhilaration of pushing his body and mind to new limits gave him a deep sense of satisfaction. But during his first marathon, he made the mistake of not properly hydrating. As he crossed the halfway point, he was still one of the top runners, but soon after, he felt intense cramps seizing his legs, unlike anything he had experienced before.

He found himself on the side of the road, massaging his calves while watching countless runners pass him. His dream of finishing strong was starting to fade. It was in this moment that an elderly man, who appeared to be his father's age, approached him and encouraged him to keep going: "Come on, son, you can do it." That encouragement, combined with the sudden surge of inspiration, gave Denis a new sense of determination.

Right then he decided that he would not let this older man pass him. He hydrated, took a deep breath, and pushed forward. With newfound energy, he picked up his stride and began passing many of the runners who had overtaken him. By the time he reached the finish line, he had not only completed the race, but he had also proven to himself that perseverance could make all the difference.

MY OWN MOMENT OF DECISION

I've had my share of moments where giving up seemed like the easiest option. When I wrote my first book, I assumed that once I finished writing, success would follow. But after completing my book, I was faced with an unexpected reality: my inventory piled up, and the sales didn't come. I found myself in debt, questioning my choices, and wondering how I could turn things around.

Then, at a seminar, a speaker made a statement that changed my life: "If you're an author, 5 percent of your job is done when you write the book; 95 percent is marketing." At that moment I decided to shift my perspective. I dove into learning everything I could about marketing my book and applying what I learned. Within months, I had sold out of my inventory, and that was the beginning of my journey of growth through online marketing. This shift was the catalyst that helped me break through my limits and achieve success in ways I never expected.

Because I didn't give up, because I chose to learn and apply everything I could about marketing, my journey didn't end with that first book. It ignited something much bigger. After my book sales began to grow and I had a few successful launches under my belt, I applied those same principles to marketing my programs, courses, services, and mentoring.

When I released my next book—and then the next, and the next after that—the momentum I built became unstoppable. With each release, I applied the lessons I learned and expanded my reach. Each book became a stepping stone to the next. Soon my books were not just successful, they were international best sellers.

What happened next was just as incredible. Authors from around the world, hearing of my success, began to reach out to me. They called, emailed, and begged for help: "Please help me," they said, "I want to know how to make my book a success like yours."

I began to teach them. I shared my journey, the mistakes I made, and the strategies that worked. It grew into one of my signature programs and has become a topic I speak about regularly on stages around the world. What started as perseverance in my own journey of book marketing blossomed into a career of teaching others how to achieve similar success.

That's not all. Because of the global nature of the Internet and the knowledge I gained in online marketing, my books eventually found their way into the hands of readers all around the world. To date, my books have been translated into approximately thirty-seven languages. And the best part? These translations and sales have occurred because there are no borders in the digital world. What once seemed like impossible reaches are now within my grasp.

Perseverance doesn't just transform your immediate results; it creates a ripple effect that opens doors and opportunities you never expected. By pushing through the challenges and staying aligned with your vision, you manifest your desires. You also create a positive impact that reaches far beyond yourself.

THE POWER OF NEVER GIVING UP

These stories are powerful reminders that the greatest successes often come right after we feel like giving up. Mark Tewksbury didn't let doubt stop him from achieving his dream. Denis chose to persist when the pain in his legs told him to stop. I made the decision to turn my book's failure into an opportunity to learn, grow, and expand my business.

It's easy to give up when things aren't going the way we expect. But the breakthroughs that lead to success often come when we choose to keep going, even when we're at our most vulnerable. These second wind moments are the ones that define us. They show us that the key to success lies in our ability to persevere, to trust in the process, and to keep moving forward.

Never, ever, ever give up. You are closer to your goal than you think. As you embrace these moments of perseverance, the Universe will meet you halfway, helping you realize the dreams you've held for so long.

18

Accomplishment through Accountability

YEARS AGO, I CAME across a study that profoundly changed the way I approached my goals. The study revealed that individuals who commit to a goal, secure an accountability partner, and check in regularly have an astonishing 95 percent likelihood of achieving their objectives. When I first heard that number, it struck me. Wouldn't you love to have a 95 percent chance of success for your biggest dreams?

Rather than just taking note of this statistic, I decided to put it into action. I found an accountability partner, and we began working together consistently. Over time, this simple yet powerful practice became a cornerstone of my personal and professional growth.

At the time of writing this book, I have an accountability partner I check in with daily. Each morning, I send an email declaring gratitude for achieving my biggest goal, even if it hasn't happened yet. My partner responds with the same level of enthusiasm and gratitude. This practice fuels my belief as well as cementing the expectation of accomplishment.

Every Sunday, I take this a step further by sending a detailed list of accomplishments to my accountability partner. However, this list isn't your typical to-do list; it's written as if everything I desire has already been completed.

For example:

"I am so happy and grateful that I completed 15,000 new words for my book this week."

"I love that I easily generated $XXXXXX in new revenue by serving incredible clients."

"I exercised every day this week for thirty minutes or more."

"I successfully recorded three additional video lessons for my new program."

The key is to frame these statements as accomplishments, not intentions. Even if I have no idea how I will achieve them when I write them down, the act of expressing gratitude in advance shifts my mindset and energy.

At the end of each week, when I send my new list of accomplishments for the upcoming week, I also include the list from the previous week. Next to each item, I add an update such as DONE, WORKING ON IT, or another brief status check. This reflection allows me to track progress without judgment. The focus is always on positivity and support. My accountability partner and I celebrate wins, encourage progress, and remain solution-oriented.

WHY THIS WORKS

Accountability adds structure to ambition. It brings clarity to the process and keeps the vision alive. Often our biggest dreams drift to the sidelines because life gets busy, distractions creep in, and self-doubt takes hold. But when you know someone is counting on you to show up, you rise to the occasion.

There is a psychological principle at play here: when we make a commitment to someone else, we are far more likely to honor it than if we only make that commitment to ourselves.

I've found that having an accountability partner enhances productivity while expanding my capacity to think bigger. There's a sense of empowerment in declaring goals out loud to someone who holds you to a higher standard.

HOW TO FIND AND WORK WITH AN ACCOUNTABILITY PARTNER

Choose someone you trust. Your accountability partner should be someone who is supportive but honest. They should hold you to your commitments without judgment or leniency.

Set a regular check-in schedule. Consistency is key. Whether it's a daily email, a weekly phone call, or a biweekly meeting, set a routine and stick to it.

Be specific and measurable. Vague goals lead to vague results. Instead of writing, "Fix my website," say, "My website is fully revised with opt-in forms working perfectly."

Celebrate wins together. Acknowledge progress, no matter how small. This reinforces the habit and keeps motivation high.

Push each other. Great accountability partners don't let you stay comfortable. They challenge you to stretch beyond your perceived limits.

PERSONAL REFLECTIONS

I've been working with an accountability partner for many years, and I credit much of my productivity and growth to this practice. It's not about bragging or keeping score; it's about staying aligned with what matters most. Some of the most significant accomplishments in my business and personal life were born from the quiet discipline of regular accountability.

I encourage you to embrace this practice wholeheartedly. Choose someone today and start small. Declare your goals, write your accomplishments as if they've already happened, and watch how the momentum builds.

In the end, accountability isn't just about getting things done. It's about achieving extraordinary things.

19

A Fresh New Start

I'VE OFTEN HEARD PEOPLE say, "If I could just start over" or "I wish I had a fresh start." The truth is, you can. In fact, you do. Every single moment is an opportunity to reset, restart, and recreate the life you desire.

Many people wait for external milestones—January 1, a birthday, or a significant life event—to declare a fresh start. But the most powerful shifts happen not by waiting for the calendar to change but by recognizing the immense potential held in the present moment. Every breath you take, every passing second, offers you a chance to step into a new version of yourself. It might seem too simple, even far-fetched, but this truth has the power to alter the course of your life.

What I'm sharing with you in this book can save you years of frustration and uncertainty. I've lived through the struggle of feeling stuck, but I've also discovered the exact tools and principles that lead to profound transformation. Now I'm giving you a shortcut. This is what some call "compressed time." What might take years to learn through trial and error, I'm handing to you now.

So let me ask you: can you grasp the power of a single moment of creation? Can you recognize that with every moment that passes, you are actively shaping your future? Each second brings you into a space of possibility and choice. The question is, how will you use this extraordinary gift? Will you focus on your desires, or will you let old stories and doubts steal the energy meant for your dreams?

Let's ground this with an example.

Imagine you're standing at the edge of a blank canvas, brush in hand. The canvas is enormous, stretching endlessly in every direction. This canvas represents your life. Some areas may already have splashes of color, but most of it remains untouched, waiting for you to make your mark.

You could stare at the canvas, overwhelmed by its vastness, thinking, "I don't even know where to start," or, "What if I make a mistake?" But here's the truth: there are no mistakes. Every stroke, every color, adds to the masterpiece. Even if you don't like what you've painted, you can pick up the brush and create anew. The canvas is never ruined.

Now imagine dipping your brush into a vibrant color that excites you—perhaps the color of joy, love, or adventure. With one simple stroke, you've begun. It's not about the whole painting coming together in an instant; it's about the courage to make that first mark.

This is the essence of starting over.

You don't need to wait for everything to be perfectly aligned. You don't need to have the entire picture figured out. You just need to take one small action—one brushstroke.

Maybe that action is writing the first page of a book, making a phone call, signing up for a class, or simply choosing to think a more empowering thought. One small act of creation begins the ripple effect.

Every day, you are standing at the edge of your canvas. The moment you decide to pick up the brush—whether it's January 1 or an ordinary Tuesday afternoon—is the moment your life begins to shift.

The mountain will wait. The canvas is always ready. Are you ready to take that first step?

20

The Bridge between Knowing and Becoming

THERE IS A PROFOUND difference between knowing what to do and doing it. In personal growth and success, the distinction between the two often marks the boundary between a life of potential and one of actualized dreams. Over the years, I've witnessed the transformation that occurs when individuals study success principles *and* choose to live them.

In this chapter, I want to introduce you to three remarkable individuals who didn't just absorb the material; they applied it. These extraordinary individuals were my clients, who immersed themselves in my programs, embraced the material, and diligently applied what they learned. Their stories highlight the power of implementation and how stepping into the *moment of creation* with unwavering belief leads to extraordinary results. Let these stories serve as inspiration and proof that the bridge between knowing and becoming is action.

DR. MARK WALLACE: RECLAIMING DREAMS AND REWRITING DESTINY

Dr. Mark Wallace's journey began with a childhood dream of becoming a novelist and screenwriter—a dream that was stifled by the limiting beliefs of others. Years later, after retiring from a long career in veterinary medicine, Dr. Mark rekindled that dream. However, it wasn't just a nostalgic wish. It became a vision he chose to embody.

The pivotal shift happened during a trip to Hollywood, where Dr. Mark met industry professionals and witnessed the real possibility of turning books into movies. For the first time, the path seemed tangible, and the pipe dream transformed into an internalized belief. Dr. Mark went beyond inspiration. He took daily action by visualizing his success every morning and night, rearranging his environment to reflect his new identity, and immersing himself in learning. His office became a sanctuary for his vision, filled with reminders of what was possible.

Dr. Mark's transformation illustrates an essential truth: aligning your environment and habits with your goals creates a continuous loop of reinforcement. He wasn't waiting for the perfect moment. He created it every day by stepping into the version of himself who had already succeeded.

WUNMI ELEBUTE: FROM LOSS TO LIMITLESS POSSIBILITIES

Wunmi's story is one of resilience and unwavering faith. When she began working with me, she was at one of the lowest points in her life. She had lost over $100,000 in an investment, leaving her with only $5,000. Despite the setback, she chose to invest part of that remaining sum into her personal growth—a decision driven by an internal nudge and a willingness to bet on herself.

Through consistent study and application, Wunmi began to reshape her identity. She didn't just listen to lessons; she lived them. She practiced gratitude for others' success, rewired limiting beliefs, and began building a new self-image. Her mantra became, "I always get what I want." This wasn't arrogance. It reflected a trust in the universe and in herself.

Wunmi documented every success, no matter how small, to build momentum. Even a free cup of coffee was celebrated as evidence that she was aligned with abundance. Over time, her reality shifted. She created businesses, launched a magazine, and witnessed opportunities flow effortlessly. Her journey underscores the power of believing in yourself even when external circumstances seem bleak.

Her life is a living testament to the idea that your external world shifts the moment you shift internally. By acting as if her success was inevitable, Wunmi brought it into form.

DR. HANAN AL MHEIRI: BUILDING AN EMPIRE FROM WITHIN

Dr. Hanan's story highlights the intersection of personal growth and professional achievement. From the loss of her mother to the dissolution of her marriage, Dr. Hanan faced a period of deep personal pain. Yet during this time she made a pivotal decision: to take full accountability for her life and create a new reality.

One of her goals was to win the Emirates Women's Award—a highly competitive and prestigious accolade. After three unsuccessful attempts, many would have walked away. Not Dr. Hanan. She refined her approach, consistently improving her submissions and using visualization techniques. She even created a mock photo of herself winning the award, fully immersing herself in the feeling of victory. When she finally won, it wasn't just in her original category—she was unexpectedly upgraded to the leadership category.

But Dr. Hanan didn't stop there. Inspired by the idea of empire building, she launched Hanan Empire—a vision she nurtured through daily practice, Power Life Scripts, and affirmations. Her alignment practices were not sporadic but woven into her daily life. Whether through intention setting or listening to recordings that reinforced her self-image, she embodied the role of Empress Hanan long before the external results manifested.

Her journey illustrates the importance of acting from the identity of the person you wish to become, not from where you currently stand.

THE COMMON THREAD: ACTION IN ALIGNMENT WITH BELIEF

While each of these stories is unique, a common thread ties them together: action rooted in belief and consistent practice. Dr. Mark, Wunmi, and Dr. Hanan didn't wait for evidence. They created the evidence through how they lived, thought, and acted.

Dr. Mark redesigned his environment and practiced visualization daily.

Wunmi celebrated small wins, rewrote her internal dialogue, and built her identity around abundance.

Dr. Hanan engaged in visualization, recorded affirmations, and lived as if her empire was already thriving.

The takeaway knowledge alone doesn't transform lives. Application does. You may already know what it takes to succeed, but are you doing it? Are you showing up every day, acting in alignment with the version of yourself that already has what you desire?

Let their examples serve as your reminder that the *moment of creation* isn't in the distant future. It is now. The individuals you've just met stand as living proof that by taking consistent, aligned action, you hold the power to reshape your reality.

You don't need to know how it will all unfold. Your responsibility is to start, believe, and keep moving forward.

TRANSFORMATION THROUGH ACTION AND COMMITMENT

The stories you've read so far exemplify the profound results that come when we move from understanding to application—from knowing to doing. But these are not isolated cases. The impact of applying what I teach extends far and wide, and the voices of countless others echo the same truth.

Dr. Durga Larkin describes how she not only gained confidence but now knows deep within that she can manifest anything she desires. Felicia Pope shares how she used these teachings to clear away debt and build wealth for her family's future.

Marian Pana had spent years immersed in personal development, but it wasn't until he experienced the depth of practical application in my programs that he found clarity. Similarly, Victoria Hirst recognizes that this work is not a one-time endeavor but a lifetime practice of self-development that continually unfolds new levels of growth.

Even those new to my teachings, like Nass Luna, express how something as simple as the realness and care in my approach created an instant connection that led to breakthroughs. Ashraf Jamie, after struggling to provide for his family, found that maintaining a positive mindset shifted everything—leading him out of financial struggle and into stability.

From Candice Stringfield, who found that the programs align perfectly with her desired growth, to Sherry Dunn, whose understanding of metaphysical principles deepened through action-oriented teachings, the message is consistent—transformation follows committed implementation.

Clients like Tessia Watson reveal that entire businesses and lifelong dreams have come to life through consistent, disciplined application of what they learned. And Michelle Snyder shares how letting go of control and trusting the process brought unexpected opportunities, including large donations to her nonprofit and the fulfillment of childhood dreams.

These are not random occurrences. They are the results of a decision to step fully into the practices, tools, and mindset shifts that create lasting success.

If you ever wonder whether success is possible for you, let these stories serve as undeniable proof. Whether it's manifesting wealth, starting a new business, or simply transforming self-doubt into unwavering belief, the principles remain the same:

- Clarity about what you desire
- Absolute belief in the possibility of that desire
- Consistent daily action and alignment with the outcome

It isn't enough to read, watch, or listen. You must embody the knowledge and put it into practice—every day, with intention and faith.

What could your life look like if you truly stepped into the application of what you already know?

Take that question into your heart as you move forward. Because the *moment of creation* is not some distant day in the future. It is now.

21

The Power of Pivotal Moments

THERE ARE MOMENTS IN life when everything shifts—when a single decision or realization becomes the catalyst for monumental transformation. These moments are often subtle at first but leave a lasting impact, rippling across every area of life. Pivotal moments are the cornerstones of growth. When embraced fully, they can lead to extraordinary breakthroughs.

In the mid-1990s, I experienced one such moment that altered the course of my life. At that point, I had already been immersed in personal development and metaphysical studies for around fifteen years. I believed in the principles I was learning, but something felt missing. I had achieved some success, but I was yearning for a quantum leap—a dramatic and lasting shift that would bring me closer to the life I envisioned.

One day, it became abundantly clear: I needed to refine my focus. I realized that while I was diligent in studying and expanding my awareness, I was still allowing too much attention to drift toward the undesirables in my life: circumstances that no longer served me, lingering regrets from the past, and fleeting worries about the future. I knew this focus was keeping me bound to the very things I wanted to change. If I wanted different results, I had to shift my gaze entirely.

I made a powerful decision to discipline my mind every single day. Not sporadically, not when it felt convenient, but as a nonnegotiable part of my daily life.

To keep myself accountable, I created something simple but profoundly effective: a Daily Discipline Tracking Sheet (a sample of which I'll provide toward the end of this book).

This checklist became my anchor. I understood that if I had a list of action items in front of me, I would follow through—one step at a time, without excuses. The checklist wasn't complex or lengthy; in fact, its simplicity was part of its power. It contained activities that aligned me with the fulfillment of my desires. Some of the core practices included:

- Daily listening to my Power Life Script
- Daily visualization of my goals and desires already fulfilled
- Expressing gratitude through written statements every morning
- Repeating affirmations in front of the mirror to reinforce positive beliefs
- Meditation and quieting the mind multiple times a day
- Reviewing my goals

By ticking off these practices each day, I systematically shifted my focus away from what I didn't want and toward what I *did* want. This created a sense of alignment and inevitability. Over time, the discipline became second nature, and the results began to show up in tangible ways.

There's something incredibly grounding about structured action. When we commit to disciplined daily practices, we build momentum that cannot be easily swayed by external circumstances. Research consistently shows that having a to-do list enhances productivity and focus. For me, the Daily Discipline Tracking Sheet was more than a productivity tool. It became a spiritual practice.

Each time I completed the list, I was reinforcing the belief that I am in control of my life. I was making deposits into the bank of my consciousness, programming my mind for success and inviting my desires to manifest with greater ease.

One of the most profound tools to emerge from this daily practice was the Power Life Script. I recognized the transformative effect of immersing myself in the feeling of my desires already fulfilled. By writing out a detailed, vivid script describing the life I desired to live, written in the present tense, and listening to it daily, I was reprogramming my subconscious mind.

This wasn't mere positive thinking. It was an immersive process of stepping into the energy and frequency of the life I desired, repeatedly and consistently, in the present moment. The more I listened, the more real it became.

Pivotal moments often require stretching beyond our comfort zones. It was uncomfortable at times to wake up earlier or to sit down and visualize when my mind wanted to drift elsewhere. There were moments of resistance, but I understood that every action taken toward my vision, no matter how small, was building a foundation for exponential growth.

Over the years, this one decision to create and adhere to a Daily Discipline Tracking Sheet became the bedrock of my success. It created ripple effects in my business, health, relationships, and financial prosperity. The small, consistent actions compounded over time, leading to breakthroughs I never could have predicted. Looking back, I can trace almost every significant leap in my life to this practice.

I often ask my clients: what one thing could you do every day that would bring you closer to your goals? The answer is usually simpler than expected. It's not about grand gestures but rather the small, repeated actions that shape our reality.

Now I invite you to reflect: Is this your pivotal moment? Are you ready to move from wishing to doing, from hoping to achieving? Perhaps you're closer to a breakthrough than you realize

Consider crafting your own Daily Discipline Tracking Sheet (or photocopy the sheet from this book). Start small. Identify a handful of practices that would align you with your desires. Commit to them daily. Allow the process to unfold.

Remember, transformation doesn't come from simply knowing the path. It comes from walking it, one step at a time.

22

Bringing the Future into the Present

AT THE CORE, THIS entire book is about one transformative principle: bringing your future desires into present reality through the power of consciousness. This practice isn't just powerful; it's the most direct path to manifesting your every desire.

Over the years, as I've conducted workshops and seminars, I've consistently woven this idea into the fabric of my teachings. Beyond explaining the concept, I love to equip my audience with practical exercises they can implement immediately. One of the most powerful exercises I share is the art of writing a future letter to yourself.

THE FUTURE LETTER EXERCISE

I guide participants to project their awareness forward: one year into the future. I ask them to imagine they are now living the life they've envisioned. Their goals have been achieved. The dream home, the soulmate, the thriving career, the financial abundance—it has all manifested beautifully. At that moment, they write to themselves from this future place of completion, detailing the joy, gratitude, and excitement they feel.

I encourage clients to write this as a heartfelt love letter to their present selves. This is not just a clinical list of achievements; it's a vivid, emotional, and deeply personal reflection of the life they've created. I remind them to focus on the emotions: to feel the satisfaction, gratitude, and pride as if it's happening right now. Here's a sample for someone manifesting their soulmate and dream home:

Dear [Your Name],

I cannot express how grateful I am to be writing this from the comfort of our dream home—the one we envisioned together for so long. Every detail is exactly as we pictured it, and it's even more beautiful in reality. The sun streams through the large windows in the mornings, and every time I walk through this house, I feel overwhelmed with gratitude. I love that we paid for it in full and it was an easy transaction. Everything fell into place magnificently.

Meeting my soulmate has been the greatest gift. Our connection is pure, joyful, and deep. We laugh endlessly, support each other, and share a vision for the future that continues to expand. I am grateful how effortlessly everything came together, but deep down, I knew this was my destiny. I trusted it. I feel so incredibly blessed and fulfilled.

Thank you for holding the vision, for believing, and for following through.

Love, [your name]

WHY THIS WORKS

Writing a future letter shifts your energy to that of completion and fulfillment. It activates the feeling of already having what you desire, which draws the experience into your life. This exercise invites you to step into alignment with the version of yourself that has already succeeded.

As with any powerful practice, it must be done consistently. Manifestation thrives on regularity. As Robert Collier said in his inspirational classic *The Secret of the Ages*: "It is not enough to know you have this power. You must put it into practice—not once, or twice, but every hour and every day."

FUTURE JOURNALING

Another powerful technique I use regularly is future journaling. I purchased a beautiful, dateless journal that allows me to choose specific days and write as if I am documenting accomplishments that have already occurred. At the start of each month, I flip to the last day and write a detailed entry reflecting on all I have achieved. It reads like a personal diary, but from the perspective of completion.

I also use this technique for specific events. If I have a speaking engagement coming up, I'll write a journal entry as if the event already happened. I'll describe the standing ovation, the positive feedback from the audience, and the joy of making an impact.

Before vacations or personal events, I journal about the ease and joy of travel, the wonderful surprises, and the smooth, delightful experience. The key is to step into the vibration of completion, allowing the subconscious mind to embrace these outcomes as inevitable.

BUILDING THE HABIT

You can easily integrate future journaling into your daily life. Pick random dates on your calendar (physical or digital) and write down affirmations and entries about the goals you wish to manifest. Write as if they have already happened. Focus on gratitude, joy, and excitement. For example:

April 15: *I'm thrilled with how our product launch turned out. The feedback has been phenomenal, and we exceeded our target by 40 percent. Our team feels more connected than ever.*

June 1: *Our relationship feels stronger and deeper every day. I'm grateful for the love, laughter, and unwavering support we share.*

STRETCHING BEYOND LIMITS

This process isn't just about achieving realistic goals. Use it to stretch beyond your comfort zone. Write down outcomes that surprise and delight you—ones that feel slightly out of reach. The more playful and expansive you allow yourself to be, the more open you are to receiving unexpected blessings.

FUTURE PROJECTION IN MASTERMIND SESSIONS

In one group of mine, I take this idea one step further. Each month, as we gather around our virtual table, I ask my clients to declare their future accomplishments for the upcoming month. This isn't just a casual exercise; it's a powerful ritual of projection and alignment.

One of my clients, Connie McIntosh, has mastered this process beautifully. Each month, she confidently declares her wins in advance, saying things like, "I have won this award," or "I have easily earned $XXXXXX," or "I have attracted XX new clients into my business." Connie's ability to quantify her future achievements is a testament to her clarity and belief. The specificity of her declarations leaves no room for ambiguity.

I always encourage my clients to stretch themselves in these sessions—to think bigger, imagine beyond their current limitations, and trust in possibilities they may not yet see. It's remarkable to witness the expansion that occurs when they commit to these future projections aloud.

By engaging in this monthly practice, my clients are consistently stepping into the version of themselves who has already succeeded. It's a simple yet transformative exercise that continually bridges the gap between desire and reality.

Future journaling, future projection, and letter writing are not meant to replace daily alignment practices, but they add fuel to the manifestation process. These techniques bridge the gap between desire and reality, pulling your vision from the intangible into the tangible.

23

Anchoring Success: The Power of Intentional Triggers

ANCHORS ARE SUBTLE YET transformative tools that help you lock in the feeling of success and alignment with your desires. While visualization, affirmations, and scripting are all effective techniques for shifting your energy, anchors provide a physical and emotional trigger that cements these practices deeper into your subconscious. They serve as reminders, pulling you back into the embodiment of your desires. When used consistently, anchors become second nature, acting as bridges between the physical and metaphysical realms.

The beauty of anchors is their simplicity. By pairing an everyday action with an intentional thought or feeling, you strengthen your belief that your desire is already yours. Anchors bypass the mind's habitual focus on current circumstances and redirect you into the state of "already achieved."

WHY ANCHORS WORK

Anchors work by creating shortcuts for the subconscious mind. Over time, these small, repeated actions build neurological pathways that reinforce the emotional state of "already having." This repetition reprograms your subconscious, dissolving doubt and allowing new beliefs to take root.

When practiced daily, anchors become embedded in your routine, gradually shifting your identity. The combination of conscious thought, physical action, and emotional alignment leads to powerful shifts in your reality.

You may already be using anchors without fully realizing their significance. Let's dive into how you can intentionally incorporate them into your daily practice.

BREATH ANCHORS: ALIGNING WITH EVERY INHALE AND EXHALE

Breathing is an unconscious act we perform thousands of times a day. By bringing awareness to our breath, we can transform it into a powerful anchor for manifestation.

Each morning, as you begin your day, breathe in with the intention of accepting your good. On the exhale, release any resistance or attachment, affirming that what you desire is already in your life. With every inhale, feel yourself receiving abundance, love, or health. As you exhale, give thanks and let go. This simple yet profound practice grounds you in certainty, reinforcing the sense that your desires are fulfilled.

Breath anchors are incredibly powerful because they allow us to bring our desires into the present moment in the simplest way possible—through our breath. But what does this look like in practice? Let me show you how to apply this technique to specific desires, transforming simple inhales and exhales into profound tools of manifestation.

Breathing in Love and Connection

Imagine someone who deeply desires to meet their soulmate. Each morning, as they sit quietly for a few minutes, they engage in intentional breathing.

Inhale (acceptance). As they draw in a long, deep breath, they close their eyes and feel the presence of love already existing in their life. They picture themselves smiling at dinner with their partner, sharing warm conversations, and feeling completely at ease in this loving connection. The inhale becomes an act of welcoming love as if it were already here.

Exhale (gratitude). As they gently release the breath, they feel immense gratitude for this relationship—the joy, laughter, and growth it brings. With each exhale, they let go of impatience or doubt, as if they're saying, "Thank you for this love I already experience."

Example thought:
Inhale. "I accept love and connection with my soulmate."
Exhale. "I am deeply grateful for the love and joy we share."

Embracing Health with Every Breath

Someone on a journey to improve their health can use breath to anchor themselves in a state of perfect well-being.

Inhale (acceptance). As they breathe in, they visualize vibrant health coursing through their veins. They feel energy radiating in their body, picturing themselves strong and full of vitality. The inhale affirms, "I am already healthy and strong."

Exhale (gratitude). As they breathe out, they silently thank their body—for the strength it provides, its healing power, and the life it sustains. Gratitude fills the space as they relax into trust, releasing worry or frustration.

Example thought:

Inhale. "I accept perfect health into every cell of my body."

Exhale. "I am grateful for the vitality and strength my body brings me."

Inviting Prosperity and Abundance

A person seeking financial growth and abundance can use each breath to anchor into wealth consciousness.

Inhale (acceptance). They breathe in deeply, imagining financial abundance flowing to them effortlessly. They see themselves enjoying the freedom and choices that come with prosperity. The inhale is an open invitation, welcoming wealth into their life.

Exhale (gratitude). As the air flows out, they focus on the blessings they already have: a roof over their head, food on the table, and opportunities that continue to appear. They breathe out gratitude, anchoring themselves in the knowing that *more* is their birthright.

Example thought:

Inhale. "I accept abundance and prosperity in my life."

Exhale. "I am grateful for the wealth and opportunities that flow to me effortlessly."

STEP ANCHORS: WALKING INTO YOUR NEW REALITY

The first step you take in the morning holds tremendous power. As you step out of bed, consciously step into the identity of the person who has already achieved their desires.

Affirm: "I am wealthy." With every step you take throughout the day, imagine you are strengthening the embodiment of success.

Affirm: "I am successful." Each footstep reinforces your belief, further anchoring you in the knowing that you are living as the highest version of yourself.

Affirm: "I am loved."

This practice transforms your walk from a mundane act into a powerful declaration of who you are choosing to be. It is a reminder that with each step, you are living your vision.

EXPANDING YOUR ANCHORS

While breath and step anchors are powerful, there are countless ways to create additional anchors that align with your desires. Below are a variety of options to explore:

Touch Anchors (Physical Cue Anchors)

Hand over Heart. Place your hand over your heart when you feel gratitude, alignment, or peace. This physical cue deepens the experience and creates a trigger that instantly reconnects you to that feeling.

Fist clench of power. Lightly clench your fist while embodying confidence and strength. This becomes a quick, physical reminder of your inner power.

Visual Anchors (Sight-Based Triggers)

Mirror affirmations. Each time you see your reflection, affirm: "I am already living my desires." This practice reinforces self-image and identity.

Auditory Anchors (Sound Triggers)

Soundtrack of success. Create audios with affirmations or guided visualization that reflects the energy of achievement. Listening to them consistently anchors the emotional state of success.

Chime or bell. Ring a small bell or chime and affirm, "It is done." This sound signals the completion and fulfillment of your desires.

Verbal Anchors (Word Triggers)

Trigger word or phrase. Choose a word or phrase like "done," "I receive," or "already mine." When spoken, it reconnects you to the feeling of completion.

Morning mantra. As you get out of bed, say aloud, "Today I live as the successful version of me."

Object Anchors (Physical Items)

Prosperity ring or bracelet. Wear a piece of jewelry that symbolizes abundance. Touching or seeing it reminds you to stay in alignment.

Sacred object. Place a meaningful object (stone, crystal, token) near you. Holding it reinforces your vision.

Writing Anchors (Mental and Physical Anchors)

Daily signature. When signing your name, mentally affirm that your signature represents someone living their highest potential.

Journaling anchor. Conclude each journal entry with "And so it is." This final statement anchors belief and completion.

Nature Anchors (Earth Connection)

Sunlight anchor. When sunlight touches your skin, acknowledge it as divine energy affirming your success.

Grounding with the earth. Standing barefoot on the earth deepens your connection to the physical world, reinforcing prosperity and abundance.

MAKING IT A PRACTICE

Choose one or two anchors to begin with and integrate them into your day. Consistency is key. Over time, you'll notice that these simple actions trigger profound states of alignment, expanding your capacity to manifest with ease.

Success is not just about knowing what to do; it's about doing it consistently. Anchors provide that bridge—a gentle yet firm nudge that reminds you to stay aligned with your highest vision.

So what anchor will you choose today?

24

One Size Does Not Fit All

IN THE JOURNEY OF personal growth and manifestation, one truth stands clear: we are not all starting from the same place. Just as no two people follow the same path to success, no two minds or hearts require identical approaches to alignment. Some of us are thriving, seeking to elevate our current success and joy. Others may feel a bit offtrack, needing a boost to get back into flow. Then there are those who feel completely disconnected, requiring a profound realignment to reconnect with their desires.

The path to alignment is not one-size-fits-all. Where you are in life will determine the approach you need to bring yourself back into balance. Recognizing where you are emotionally, mentally, and spiritually will help you apply the right tools that lead to transformation.

Your alignment process is unique to you. Understanding whether you need daily maintenance, a quick reset, or deeper immersion is essential to creating the results you desire. The practices you use and the tools you apply should align with where you are in the moment.

YOUR JOURNEY, YOUR BLUEPRINT

Over the years, I've learned that true transformation happens when we meet ourselves where we are. Many make the mistake of trying to apply the same approach to everyone, unaware that the tools that work for one person may not be what's needed at a given moment.

Through this book, I invite you to understand where you stand emotionally and mentally so you can use the tools that work best for your current state. Your journey and your blueprint are yours to define. By using the right tools at the right time, you will create lasting change.

EMPOWERING REFLECTION

Take a moment to reflect on your current state:

Do you feel mostly aligned but want to expand further?

Are you slightly out of alignment, needing small yet powerful shifts?

Do you feel completely offtrack, as if you've lost connection to your dreams?

By answering these questions honestly, you're taking the first step in personal transformation. Understanding where you are right now will help you implement the most effective practices.

THE ROAD AHEAD

In the next chapter, "The Alignment Blueprint," you'll find tools and practices tailored for each stage of alignment. Whether you need daily maintenance, a quick reset, or profound immersion, there is a practice designed specifically for you. By applying the right tools at the right time, you unlock your path to greater ease, confidence, and clarity.

Remember, you are your own guide. You have everything you need to realign and move forward on your unique path.

No one stays aligned all day long, and that's OK. What matters is being prepared—ready to switch from doubt to belief, from fear to trust, and from disconnection to alignment. With these tools, you can keep moving forward, one aligned step at a time.

25

Alignment Self-Assessment Quiz

Welcome to a fun and enlightening process! This quiz will help you discover your current state of alignment and choose the path that best supports your flow. Answer the following questions honestly and intuitively. This is not about judgment: this is about awareness. The results will guide you toward the most effective alignment plan, allowing you to take the next steps with ease. (We'll go into the different alignment plans in the next chapter.)

1. How often do you feel in flow with your desires?
    A. Almost daily.
    B. Occasionally, but not consistently.
    C. Rarely. I often feel disconnected or out of sync.

2. When you think about your goals or dreams, how do you feel?
    A. Excited and confident.
    B. Hopeful, but sometimes doubtful.
    C. Frustrated, anxious, or overwhelmed.

3. How quickly do you recover from negative emotions like doubt or frustration?
    A. Quickly. I can shift my mindset within minutes or hours.
    B. It varies, but I usually bounce back within a day or two.
    C. I often stay stuck in negative emotions for days or longer.

4. How connected do you feel to your intuition or inner guidance?
    A. Strongly connected. I trust my inner voice.
    B. Somewhat connected, but I sometimes second-guess myself.
    C. Disconnected. I often feel lost or unsure.

5. When challenges arise, how do you typically respond?
    A. I trust the process and stay focused on solutions.
    B. I feel the challenge but try to remain hopeful.
    C. I get overwhelmed or feel like giving up.

6. How consistent are you with daily practices like affirmations, visualization, or gratitude?
    A. I practice daily without fail.
    B. I practice sporadically, depending on how I feel.
    C. I struggle to maintain a consistent routine.

7. Do you find yourself frequently comparing your progress to that of others?
    A. Rarely. I stay focused on my own path.
    B. Sometimes, but I try not to let it affect me.
    C. Often, and it leaves me feeling behind or inadequate.

SCORING YOUR RESULTS

Mostly A's. You are generally in alignment, but to keep your flow, consistent daily practices are key. This plan focuses on sustaining your natural flow and maintaining ease and alignment in your life. *Daily practices plan: natural flow.*

Mostly B's. You experience alignment at times but may occasionally feel disconnected. A quick reset will help you realign. This plan is designed for moments of recalibration, where you return to alignment with brief, intentional practices. *Quick reset plan: the reset room.*

Mostly C's. You may be feeling significantly out of alignment. This is an opportunity for deep, transformative realignment. A more immersive, focused approach is recommended to guide you back into flow, creating lasting change. *Deep transformation plan: the immersion.*

NEXT STEPS

Once you've identified your alignment plan, turn to the corresponding section of the next chapter to begin your realignment journey.

This quiz is simply a tool for awareness. As life evolves, you can shift between plans depending on your desires and progress. Trust that you always have the power to realign at any time.

Your awareness of where you stand is the first step to guiding yourself toward where you wish to be.

26

The Alignment Blueprint

THE JOURNEY TO ALIGNMENT is as unique as you are. Just as every individual has their own path to health and wellness, your journey to inner harmony requires a personalized blueprint. As we've seen, there is no one-size-fits-all solution, and that's the beauty of it. Whether you're feeling mostly aligned and want to maintain your flow or you're experiencing a disconnect and need to realign, the first step is understanding where you are right now and then choosing the right practices to bring you back into balance.

Your alignment plan will evolve depending on where you are at the moment. The key is to remember that these tools are not only for times of crisis or imbalance; they're essential to keep you in alignment even during the smooth times. Whether you're feeling deeply connected or need to course-correct, these practices will keep you on the path to realizing your desires.

YOUR ALIGNMENT PATH
There are three basic levels of alignment:

Natural flow: daily alignment practices. This is for the person who feels good but desires to maintain or enhance their flow. These daily practices, simple and consistent, help you stay aligned and keep your energy flowing aligned with your desires.

Quick reset: instant realignment. We all experience moments of misalignment. When doubts arise or frustrations build, quick resets are essential. These simple practices allow you to realign and regain your focus.

Immersion: deep realignment for transformation. When you feel deeply disconnected from your desires or overwhelmed by life, a more immersive approach is necessary. Deep realignment requires time, commitment, and focus, allowing for lasting transformation and reconnection to your highest self.

DESIGNING YOUR ALIGNMENT BLUEPRINT
In this chapter, I'll guide you through creating your personal Alignment Blueprint. Think of it as a roadmap that ensures that your thoughts, feelings, and actions are always in perfect harmony with the life you are manifesting.

WHERE ARE YOU RIGHT NOW?

Before diving into your Alignment Blueprint, take a moment to reflect on how you're feeling. Ask yourself:

Do you feel mostly aligned but need some fine-tuning to maintain your flow?

Are you occasionally knocked off course by doubt, frustration, or external stressors?

Or do you feel disconnected, in need of a full reset to realign with your highest desires?

Your answers will guide you toward the blueprint that best suits your needs right now. Once you've identified where you are, you can choose the path that resonates most.

THREE ALIGNMENT PATHS

Path 1:
Natural Flow: Daily Alignment Practices

Purpose: To maintain your alignment and prevent small misalignments from interrupting your flow.

Just as you need daily nutrition and rest, your alignment plan requires regular attention. Daily practices are the key to maintaining the flow of energy and keeping your desires in perfect harmony with your life.

For those who are generally in alignment but want to keep their energy flowing smoothly, this is your daily routine, consisting of simple, preventive practices that ensure you stay on track. Think of it as your daily spiritual hygiene.

Your practice:

Morning activation. Start your day with three deep breaths. Breathe in acceptance and exhale gratitude (use the breath anchor technique as shared earlier in the book). Set a clear intention for the day. How would you love your day to go? What positive and supportive energy do you want to carry with you throughout the day?

Visualization. Visualize your dream life and immerse yourself in the emotions of living it right now, in this very moment.

Affirmations. Speak your affirmations aloud to reinforce your alignment. Words carry energy and intention. Make them powerful.

Repetition of impressions. Listen to your Power Life Script in the morning and at night before you sleep. Let these positive words penetrate deeply into your subconscious mind.

Gratitude journaling. Upon waking and/or before bed, reflect on five things you're grateful for. This simple practice keeps your focus on abundance and sets the tone for the next day.

Path 2:
Quick Reset: Instant Realignment for Off Days

Purpose: To quickly regain alignment when negative emotions or distractions arise.

Everyone experiences moments of misalignment, but the key is to realign quickly before small issues snowball into bigger challenges. A quick reset can bring you back into balance, just like grabbing the wheel when the car starts veering off course. These quick practices are for moments when you're not feeling quite right—when something feels off and you need to recalibrate quickly. They will help you shift your energy and realign with your highest self.

Your reset:

Grounding breathwork. Take five grounding breaths. Inhale deeply, imagining golden light filling your body, and exhale any tension or resistance. Feel the weight of your body reconnecting with the earth.

Gratitude reset. Acknowledge three things that are currently going well in your life. Gratitude is a powerful tool to shift your energy back into alignment.

Minivisualization. Close your eyes and visualize your end goal for two minutes. Feel the joy and satisfaction of its completion. The more vividly you can imagine it, the more powerful your reset.

Affirmation or mantra. Use a statement like, "I am safe. I am aligned. All is well." Repeat it whenever you feel the need to realign.

Repetition of Impressions. Listen to your Power Life Script. Allow the words to recalibrate your energy and bring you back to your center.

Empowering questions. Ask yourself, "What would I love right now?" or "Now that I am living my dreams, how do I feel?"

Path 3:
Immersion: Deep Realignment for Transformation

Purpose: For profound realignment and emotional resets during deep disconnects or periods of intense transformation.

Sometimes a full reset is necessary. If you're feeling disconnected, emotionally drained, or in a state of transformation, immersion in powerful alignment practices is key. This path is for those ready for profound inner work to restore balance and elevate their energy. Commit to the deep inner work that will restore your energy and elevate your alignment.

Your immersion:

Full immersion visualization. Dedicate thirty to sixty minutes to a deeply immersive visualization practice. See your desires unfolding in full color, and feel the emotions of success, abundance, and joy as though it's happening right now.

Extended breathwork. Practice fifteen to thirty minutes of deep breathwork using the breath anchoring technique. Inhale deeply, filling your lungs with fresh energy, and exhale slowly, expressing gratitude. This invites positive energy to flow through you.

Mirror work. Stand in front of a mirror and affirm your desires as though they are already fulfilled. Look into your eyes and feel the truth of your statements. This practice helps shift your self-image and align your energy with your highest potential. Claim: "I am so relaxed knowing that . . ."

Repetition of impressions. Listen to your Power Life Script multiple times today, truly connecting with the words and feeling the emotion behind them.

Disconnect to reconnect. Take a break from external distractions such as social media, the news, or other people's opinions. Use this time to reconnect with your inner truth and realign your energy.

YOUR ALIGNMENT BLUEPRINT

Now it's your turn. Reflect on the following:

What practices will you commit to daily to maintain your alignment?

How will you realign when you feel off or disconnected?

What will your "deep dive" immersion look like when you need profound transformation?

Write your answers down and treat this as a commitment to yourself. This is your personalized guide to staying in alignment with your highest desires. Keep it with you and refer to it as needed. As you grow, so will your Alignment Blueprint.

Trust that the right tools for your alignment are always available when you need them. Your path to alignment is yours to define. Embrace it with confidence, knowing that each step brings you closer to the life you are meant to live.

Staying aligned is not about perfection. It's about having the tools ready when you need them most. Whether it's through asking the right questions, affirming your truth, visualizing your desires, or using your Power Life Script, these tools allow you to make a quick mental switch that realigns you with your highest self.

No one stays aligned all day long, and that's OK. What matters is being armed and ready—ready to switch from doubt to belief, from fear to trust, and from disconnection to alignment. With these tools in your arsenal, you have everything you need to keep moving forward, one aligned step at a time.

27

Creating with Ease and Flow

As we've explored throughout this book, life is not meant to be a struggle. There's a profound truth in the idea that creation should not be an arduous battle, but a joyful, flowing process. In fact, one of the most transformative shifts you can make on your journey to manifesting your ideal life is to embrace the idea of ease—the art of creating with minimal effort, by simply allowing what is meant to come to you.

THE POWER OF LETTING GO

One of the most powerful lessons I've learned in my life is the importance of letting go. For years, I believed that I had to struggle, to push, to fight for what I wanted. It wasn't until I consciously chose to let go of this mindset that everything began to shift. I created a theme for my year: "Relax." I placed *relax* signs all around my home as a constant reminder to rest in the knowing that everything

I desired was already done. This simple action allowed the flow of abundance and ease to flood into my life.

As I made relaxation my theme, I also changed all my goal statements to say, "I am relaxed in the knowing . . ." This small but powerful shift helped me embrace a state of ease instead of anxiety or striving. I also ensured that I meditated every single day. These practices completely transformed my life. No more struggle. No more stress. And most importantly, a huge amount of *allowing*.

THE PRINCIPLE OF LEAST EFFORT

The principle of least effort is a core component of allowing ease into your life. This is not about being passive or lazy; it's about being in alignment with the natural flow of life. When we allow things to unfold naturally, we don't need to force them into existence. Effortlessness is a result of trust and surrender—trust that the universe has a plan for us and surrendering to the process.

In this moment, you can choose to step into the flow and allow things to happen with grace. It's about letting go of the need to push and instead allowing life to unfold with ease. This is where the magic happens. When you stop forcing, life can unfold in miraculous ways.

RELAXING INTO YOUR DESIRES

One key takeaway from earlier chapters is that life is not meant to be a battle. Creating your desires does not have to involve struggle. Remember when we discussed denying the evidence of the senses and how practice makes this easier? The same goes for allowing ease into your life. We are habitual beings, and once we create new habits—habits of ease, habits of allowing—everything begins to flow better. The more you practice relaxing into the knowing, the more effortless it becomes to create your reality.

Allowing your desires to come to you means trusting that you don't have to chase them down. Instead, relax, let go, and receive. It is all available to you now. When you align with ease, you are opening the door to your desires in a way that feels natural and true.

TRUST AND SURRENDER

If you've been following along in this book, you know that *life does not have to be hard*. The battles we think we need to fight don't always exist. By embracing ease, you can surrender to the flow of life, which brings you everything you need, at the perfect time, in the perfect way. Allow yourself to trust in the process.

One of the most powerful moments in my life came years ago when someone asked me, "Are you willing to have your life go well all the time?" At first, I thought it was a trick question, as if there was a catch. But as I sat with it, I realized that the answer had to be *yes*. Saying yes to having your life go well all the time is an invitation to ease. It is a declaration that you are willing to release struggle and accept the natural flow of abundance that is available to you.

PRACTICING EASE IN DAILY LIFE

Now that we've explored the concepts of relaxing into your desires, allowing ease, and trusting the process, how can you practice these on a daily basis?

1. **Set an intention of ease.** Each day, set the intention to create with ease. Say to yourself, "I am relaxed in the knowing that

everything I desire is already mine." Allow this intention to guide your thoughts and actions throughout the day.
2. **Release control.** Notice where you're trying to control outcomes or force situations. Practice letting go of that control, and simply allow things to unfold as they will.
3. **Meditate or breathe.** Meditation, or even a few minutes of deep breathing, can help you reconnect with ease. Meditation allows you to quiet the mind, release stress, and invite flow into your life.
4. **Trust the process.** Remind yourself that everything is working in your favor, even when it doesn't appear that way. Trust that the universe is guiding you to where you need to be.
5. **Practice gratitude.** By focusing on what is going well in your life and being thankful for it, you create more room for ease and flow.

THE ART OF ALLOWING EASE

Life does not need to be a struggle. Creating your desires can be a simple, effortless process. By embracing ease, relaxing into the knowing, and trusting the process, you open the door to greater abundance, joy, and fulfillment. This is not a theory. It's a practical way of living that will change your life.

Your ideal life is waiting for you. It's already here. All you have to do is allow it to unfold.

28

The Ultimate Moment of Creation: Living as if It Is Already Done

THERE COMES A POINT in every journey when the tools are no longer the focus—you are. The practices, the affirmations, the visualizations all serve a singular purpose: to bring you into alignment with the truth that what you desire is already yours. But the ultimate moment of creation isn't a fleeting experience; it's a state of being.

This chapter isn't about teaching you something new. It's an invitation to step fully into the identity of the creator you were born to be. The shift you seek is not waiting for the right conditions. It doesn't depend on how many affirmations you repeat or how long you visualize. It is here. Now.

LIVING AS IF

To live as if your desires are already fulfilled means to carry the energy of completion in everything you do. It means walking, speaking, and breathing in alignment with the belief that your creation is already done.

Imagine this:

You wake up in the morning and smile, not because your desires are coming, but because they are already here.

You feel gratitude not as a tool to attract something, but because you know you are living in the results of your deepest dreams.

Every action you take is a reflection of the person who already has it.

This is the shift that unlocks the floodgates.

THE POWER OF "DONE"

One of the most transformative beliefs you can hold is "it is already done." By affirming that your desires exist in the now, you collapse the gap between dreaming and receiving.

When you reach the point where you no longer ask when or how, but live from the certainty that it already *is*, you unlock the most powerful moment of creation.

EXERCISE

Close your eyes. Imagine your greatest desire as if it has already happened. Don't just see it—feel it. Breathe as the version of you who has already manifested this reality. Let your body relax into the sensation of knowing.

Let this become your daily practice: a continuous return to the truth that what you desire is not outside of you. It is already within, fully formed, simply waiting for you to claim it.

Epilogue

Your Creation Is Already Done

As you turn this page, remember: you are not the person who picked up this book. You are no longer someone searching for answers. The answers are within you. You are no longer someone who waits for miracles. You *are* the miracle.

Your journey from awakening to action has brought you here, to this moment. And this moment is the most powerful one you will ever have—because it is the only moment. Creation does not exist in the future. It exists now.

As you step forward from these words, let your next breath be a declaration:

"I create effortlessly. My desires are already fulfilled. I am living the life I envisioned, right here, right now."

Let this be your mantra. Let this be the frequency you embody every day. Breathe it in. Walk with it. Live from it.

The universe responds to certainty. And you, dear reader, are the creator of your reality. This is your moment. This is your masterpiece.

The *moment of creation* is not coming. It is here.

Bonus Chapter

Tools for Daily Success and Alignment

IN THIS BONUS CHAPTER, I am thrilled to share two of the most life-changing tools that have transformed my journey as well as the journeys of countless others. These tools are powerful, but they are only effective if you use them. *They have no value unless you use them consistently.*

When I first discovered the power of intentional tracking and daily discipline, something shifted for me. It was as if I was finally given the blueprint to align my thoughts, feelings, and actions with my desires in a way that allowed them to manifest quickly and effortlessly. But here's the secret: it wasn't the tools themselves that brought me results: it was my commitment to using them every single day. I made a decision to show up for myself and put in the work, and that's when I saw everything begin to change.

These tools reflect the principles you've already been introduced to in this book. They're designed to keep you in alignment with your goals, help you track your emotional and energetic state, and ensure you're taking the consistent actions necessary to create the life you desire. But, as with any tool, their true value comes from regular use and dedication. It's not about using them once and expecting instant results; it's about consistently applying them to your daily life.

THE VIBRATIONAL ALIGNMENT TRACKING SHEET

When I first started using the Vibrational Alignment Tracking Sheet, I was amazed at how simple it was to check in with myself throughout the day. I used to go about my business without really paying attention to where my energy was focused, but this tool made me more aware of the subtle shifts in my emotions and thoughts.

By tracking my emotional state regularly, I was able to recognize when I was slipping into negative energy or doubting my desires. More importantly, I could immediately shift my focus back to the positive, realigned energy that supported my goals. This awareness was key to accelerating my manifestation process. When I began to track my energy, I realized how much my emotions were dictating my results.

If you're ready for big changes in your life, I encourage you to use this sheet every day. Set aside time—whether it's hourly or in a few moments during the day—to check in with yourself. See where your energy is and course-correct when necessary. Through this consistent practice, you'll experience the power of true alignment.

THE DAILY DISCIPLINE TRACKING SHEET

The Daily Discipline Tracking Sheet is a perfect companion to the Vibrational Alignment Sheet. While alignment focuses on your internal state and emotions, discipline ensures that you're taking the right actions every day to support your goals. *Daily disciplines are the bridge between your vision and your results.*

When I started using this tool, it felt like a game changer. I could clearly track my daily actions and see where I was putting my time and energy. Was I staying aligned with the vision of my future, or was I distracted? Was I moving forward, or was I getting stuck in procrastination or doubt? This sheet forced me to get real with myself and take ownership of my actions.

Here's the truth: results don't come from wishes, they come from consistent, aligned actions. Just like building a muscle, the more you use the Daily Discipline Tracking Sheet, the stronger your results will become. It's about showing up every day, doing the work, and watching your dreams unfold.

HOW THESE TOOLS WORK TOGETHER

These tools are not just tasks to be completed. They are practices that align your mindset, emotions, and actions. They are the compass that keeps you on course when things feel uncertain. The Vibrational Alignment Tracking Sheet keeps your energy in check, and the Daily Discipline Tracking Sheet ensures that you're taking the necessary steps to manifest your goals.

It's easy to get caught up in the idea that something will change overnight. But real change comes when we commit to the process.

These tools are a part of that process. They work together to create a sustainable, powerful approach to manifestation.

FINAL THOUGHTS ON THE TOOLS

I've seen firsthand how powerful these tools can be. The results I've experienced—and the results of my clients—are a direct result of using these tools consistently. When you apply them, you'll see your desires begin to manifest more effortlessly.

Just like anything else, these tools only work if you use them. Your commitment to the process will determine the speed and power with which your desires materialize. It's about showing up, doing the work, and trusting that the Universe is always responding to you.

Take these tools, use them daily, and watch how your life transforms.

VIBRATIONAL ALIGNMENT *Tracking Sheet*

Your Goal: _____

Use this sheet to track your vibrational alignment throughout the day. Every hour, pause and reflect on your current alignment with your desires, noting your thoughts, feelings, and energy level. This will help you remain conscious of your state and adjust as needed.

Discipline	Time Current Feeling/Emotion	Aligned or Not Aligned?	Notes/Adjustments
6:00 a.m.			
7:00 a.m.			
8:00 a.m.			
9:00 a.m.			
10:00 a.m.			
11:00 a.m.			
12:00 p.m.			
1:00 p.m.			
2:00 p.m.			
3:00 p.m.			
4:00 p.m.			
5:00 p.m.			
6:00 p.m.			
7:00 p.m.			
8:00 p.m.			
9:00 p.m.			
10:00 p.m.			

INSTRUCTIONS:

✓ Set an hourly reminder alarm to pause and check your alignment.

✓ At each check-in, reflect on your current state. Are your thoughts in harmony with your desires? Are you feeling emotions that align with the outcome you seek (e.g., gratitude, joy, peace)? Are your actions and decisions in alignment with your goals?

✓ Record your alignment status and any adjustments or actions you'll take to shift into a higher vibration if needed.

REFLECTION AT DAY'S END:

Overall Alignment Today (Rate Yourself Scale 1–10): _____

What worked well? _____

What will I improve for tomorrow? _____

VIBRATIONAL ALIGNMENT *Weekly Tracking*

Focus: _____

Monday		Tuesday		Wednesday		Thursday	
Time	Aligned	Time	Aligned	Time	Aligned	Time	Aligned
6:00 a.m.		6:00 a.m.		6:00 a.m.		6:00 a.m.	
7:00 a.m.		7:00 a.m.		7:00 a.m.		7:00 a.m.	
8:00 a.m.		8:00 a.m.		8:00 a.m.		8:00 a.m.	
9:00 a.m.		9:00 a.m.		9:00 a.m.		9:00 a.m.	
10:00 a.m.		10:00 a.m.		10:00 a.m.		10:00 a.m.	
11:00 a.m.		11:00 a.m.		11:00 a.m.		11:00 a.m.	
12:00 p.m.		12:00 p.m.		12:00 p.m.		12:00 p.m.	
1:00 p.m.		1:00 p.m.		1:00 p.m.		1:00 p.m.	
2:00 p.m.		2:00 p.m.		2:00 p.m.		2:00 p.m.	
3:00 p.m.		3:00 p.m.		3:00 p.m.		3:00 p.m.	
4:00 p.m.		4:00 p.m.		4:00 p.m.		4:00 p.m.	
5:00 p.m.		5:00 p.m.		5:00 p.m.		5:00 p.m.	
6:00 p.m.		6:00 p.m.		6:00 p.m.		6:00 p.m.	
7:00 p.m.		7:00 p.m.		7:00 p.m.		7:00 p.m.	
8:00 p.m.		8:00 p.m.		8:00 p.m.		8:00 p.m.	
9:00 p.m.		9:00 p.m.		9:00 p.m.		9:00 p.m.	
10:00 p.m.		10:00 p.m.		10:00 p.m.		10:00 p.m.	

Friday		Saturday		Sunday	
Time	Aligned	Time	Aligned	Time	Aligned
6:00 a.m.		6:00 a.m.		6:00 a.m.	
7:00 a.m.		7:00 a.m.		7:00 a.m.	
8:00 a.m.		8:00 a.m.		8:00 a.m.	
9:00 a.m.		9:00 a.m.		9:00 a.m.	
10:00 a.m.		10:00 a.m.		10:00 a.m.	
11:00 a.m.		11:00 a.m.		11:00 a.m.	
12:00 p.m.		12:00 p.m.		12:00 p.m.	
1:00 p.m.		1:00 p.m.		1:00 p.m.	
2:00 p.m.		2:00 p.m.		2:00 p.m.	
3:00 p.m.		3:00 p.m.		3:00 p.m.	
4:00 p.m.		4:00 p.m.		4:00 p.m.	
5:00 p.m.		5:00 p.m.		5:00 p.m.	
6:00 p.m.		6:00 p.m.		6:00 p.m.	
7:00 p.m.		7:00 p.m.		7:00 p.m.	
8:00 p.m.		8:00 p.m.		8:00 p.m.	
9:00 p.m.		9:00 p.m.		9:00 p.m.	
10:00 p.m.		10:00 p.m.		10:00 p.m.	

INSTRUCTIONS:

Place a checkmark beside each hour, each day, to confirm you ARE in alignment with your desire(s).

DAILY DISCIPLINE *Tracking Sheet*

My Goal is: _____

I am committed to these new disciplines every day and will follow through with total enthusiasm, focus and gratitude.

Sign here: _____

Discipline	Monday	Tuesday	Wednesday	Thursday	Friday	Saturday	Sunday

Discipline	Monday	Tuesday	Wednesday	Thursday	Friday	Saturday	Sunday

Discipline	Monday	Tuesday	Wednesday	Thursday	Friday	Saturday	Sunday

Discipline	Monday	Tuesday	Wednesday	Thursday	Friday	Saturday	Sunday

Discipline	Monday	Tuesday	Wednesday	Thursday	Friday	Saturday	Sunday

Bonus Chapter

Your Daily Decree for Embracing the *Moment of Creation*

As you reach the final pages of this book, I want to leave you with a powerful practice that will continue to guide you on your journey of creation. This decree is a daily tool that anchors you in the truth of who you are—the creator of your reality. It is designed to remind you of your limitless potential and keep you grounded in the present moment, where all possibilities exist.

By affirming this decree each day, you reaffirm your alignment with the life you desire to create. It becomes your daily ritual, a constant reminder of the powerful energy that flows within you and the life that you are manifesting right now. Allow it to be a living, breathing part of your experience, and know that with every word, you are stepping further into the *moment of creation*.

HOW TO USE THE DECREE

Read it aloud each morning. Start your day by reading the decree aloud. Speaking it aloud helps anchor the energy and power of the words within you. Feel each affirmation as if it is already true. Let the words resonate deeply within your being.

Visualize as you speak. As you read the decree, close your eyes and visualize your desires already fulfilled. Picture the life you want to create, seeing it as vividly and clearly as possible. Imagine yourself living fully aligned with your highest self, feeling the joy, peace, and abundance that come with it.

Write it down. For added impact, write the decree down each day. Writing helps to reinforce the message in your subconscious mind. You can keep a journal or notebook specifically for this purpose. Let this practice become an anchor for your day.

Use it whenever you need a boost. If you feel misaligned, uncertain, or offtrack during the day, take a moment to read the decree again. Let it center you and return you to the present moment. It's a quick, easy way to realign your thoughts, feelings, and energy.

Affirm it before bed. Before you go to sleep, recite the decree one more time. Let the words settle deeply into your subconscious as you rest. Allow it to become your truth while you sleep, so your mind can continue to work on your alignment even as you rest.

Print and place it where you can see it. Print the decree and place it somewhere you'll see it every day—on your mirror, by your bed, or at your desk. Let it be a constant reminder that you are living in the *moment of creation*, fully aligned with the life you are manifesting.

THE *MOMENT OF CREATION* DECREE

I am the creator of my reality, and I live in the power of this moment.

I stand fully aligned with the infinite possibilities of the present.

I embrace my inner power and choose to manifest my desires with ease and grace.

Every thought, word, and action flows in perfect harmony with the life I love.

I know that my success is absolutely guaranteed.

I am worthy of all the good I experience, and it is already reflected in my life.

Abundance flows freely and easily to me, and I receive it with open arms.

I trust in the divine order of life, and all is perfectly unfolding.

I am a magnet for success, love, and joy, and they are the natural expression of who I am.

I am grateful for every moment, knowing that each one is a gift filled with limitless potential.

I radiate peace, love, and abundance, and they surround me in every way.

I live in full alignment with my highest self, embodying the truth that I am whole, I am complete, and I am living my best life now.

I am relaxed in the knowing that everything I desire is already mine.

I declare that the *moment of creation* is here, and I am fully present in it, making every moment count.

I love my life and every part of it, giving thanks every day.

Addendum

Anchored in the Words of Creation

THROUGHOUT *The Moment of Alignment*, you've been guided to recognize the immense power that exists within you—the power to manifest, align, and bring your deepest desires to life. The quotes in this addendum are not just words; they are anchors—reminders that creation is not an event, but a continuous unfolding.

Each quote reflects the book's core message: that your reality is shaped by the thoughts you hold, the emotions you embody, and the unwavering faith you cultivate in the unseen. These words are intended to serve as daily touchstones, pulling you back into alignment whenever you feel disconnected from your desires.

Let this addendum be more than just a collection of phrases. Let it be a source of power, a return to center, and a guidepost for the life you are creating. Revisit these words often, allow them to sink deeply into your consciousness, and use them as fuel to stay anchored in the moment of creation.

The path is yours. The moment is now.

THE POWER OF NOW AND ALIGNMENT

- Creation is not a one-time event or distant memory. It's happening now, in every thought we think, every emotion we feel, and every choice we make.
- Your ideal life is not somewhere in the future. It's already yours, ready to be realized—right now.
- The most powerful moment in our lives is not some distant memory of the past or a dream of the future. It is the moment of *now*—the *moment of creation*.
- Magic begins when we direct our thoughts with intention, align with our desires, and embrace the present moment.
- What you focus on grows. Where you invest your attention, your energy flows.
- Anchoring yourself in the present moment is the fastest way to shift the trajectory of your future.
- Alignment isn't something you achieve once and forget. It is a daily practice, a commitment to living in harmony with your highest self.

ON FAITH, BELIEF, AND OVERCOMING RESISTANCE

- Faith is the bridge that carries us from doubt to certainty, from scarcity to abundance.
- Resistance often shows up strongest just before the breakthrough. When you feel like giving up, keep going.
- Your desires manifest the moment you feel them as already fulfilled.

- When you deny the evidence of the senses and trust in the unseen, you unlock the doors to limitless potential.
- True creation begins when we realize that the invisible realm of our thoughts shapes our visible reality.
- Doubt delays manifestation. Faith accelerates it.
- Let go of *how* and focus on *what*. The universe handles the details when you stay anchored in faith.
- Live in the certainty of your dreams as if they are already your reality—and they will be.
- Success flows to those who hold unwavering belief, even in the absence of visible proof.

MANIFESTING LOVE AND ABUNDANCE

- Love, abundance, and joy are not things we wait for. They are states of being we choose to step into.
- Manifesting love begins with deciding you are worthy of it, feeling it, and aligning with it in every moment.
- Abundance is not something to chase: it's something to accept and allow.
- By focusing on the feeling of having what you desire, you naturally draw it toward you.
- Your reality is not defined by external circumstances, but by the story you tell yourself each day.
- The universe responds to the energy you emit. When you embody the feeling of your desires already fulfilled, the universe conspires to make it so.
- Your thoughts shape your future, but your feelings anchor it into being.

GRATITUDE AND APPRECIATION AS CATALYSTS

- Appreciation is the gateway to abundance. What you appreciate multiplies in your life.
- Gratitude shifts your focus from what's missing to what's present, opening the door for more blessings to enter.
- The fastest way to realign with your desires is to appreciate what you already have.
- When you live in a state of gratitude, even the smallest moments become extraordinary.
- The more you celebrate the present, the more life gives you to celebrate.
- Gratitude in advance is one of the most powerful forces in creation. Feel the joy of receiving before it arrives, and it will come faster than you can imagine.

RESILIENCE AND RISING ABOVE CHALLENGES

- It's not the absence of challenges that defines our success; it's our ability to rise above them.
- The path to alignment isn't always smooth, but even in moments of doubt, returning to your vision realigns you.
- Your greatest growth happens in the moments you choose faith over fear.
- Every challenge holds within it the seed of greater strength and transformation.
- Trust that everything is working out, even if the evidence hasn't yet appeared.

ON CREATION AND INFINITE POTENTIAL

- Creation begins the moment you accept your desire as an already accomplished fact.
- The universe rearranges itself the moment you declare what you truly want.
- Your imagination is the blueprint of your future. Guard it, nurture it, and expand it.
- The seeds of everything you desire are already planted within you. Your job is to water them with belief and action.
- The invisible is more real than the visible. Your thoughts shape worlds long before your hands do.

STEPPING INTO YOUR POWER

- You don't need permission to create the life you desire—only a decision.
- Power flows where clarity exists. The clearer you are on your desires, the faster they manifest.
- Your desires are not random; they are whispers from the part of you that knows what's possible.
- You are the architect of your life. Build with intention, or you'll construct someone else's design by default.
- What you accept as possible sets the boundaries of your reality. Expand your belief, and your world expands with it.

ON ACTION AND MOMENTUM

- Inspired action is the bridge between your desires and their manifestation.

- Act as if your desire is already yours. This accelerates its arrival.
- Small, consistent steps compound into extraordinary results.
- Action taken from alignment outpaces hard work taken from fear.
- Your journey begins the moment you stop hesitating and fully step into the energy of the life you want.

TRUSTING THE PROCESS

- Trust that the same force that spins the planets is guiding your desires into form.
- Let go of the *how*. Focus on the *what*, and the path will reveal itself.
- Even if you can't see it yet, know that the wheels of creation are turning in your favor.
- Your job isn't to push the river; it's to flow with it.
- Patience isn't waiting: it's trusting the unfolding.

Acknowledgments

I WANT TO BEGIN by acknowledging the most important people in my life: my immediate family, whose love, support, and inspiration shape who I am every single day. First, my husband, Denis. I often say I won the lottery when I met and married him, and that is still the truth. He is the most wonderful man, and I thank him every day for the joy and love he brings into my life.

I'm deeply grateful for my son, Michel, who is a constant source of pride. He has always been the greatest gift in my life. His determination and commitment to his goals—like creating his own successful business within its first year—serve as a true testament to his character. He is a risk taker who knows how to win. I'm thrilled to watch him succeed in every way.

I am equally thankful for my daughter-in-law, Kayla, not just as a member of my family but also as a major contributor in my business, Dynamic Destinies Inc. Kayla's philosophy of bringing greater value to the world aligns perfectly with the values I hold dear. She has a spirit like those of many successful people I've written about in this book. I know that she will continue to be recognized for her positive impact.

My grandson, James, is a blessing in my life. His kindness, love, and generosity are unmatched. His talent on the piano moves me deeply, and I am amazed by his extraordinary abilities. My granddaughter, Aria, is a force to be reckoned with in the most positive way. She is funny, loving, and incredibly driven. If she wants something, she'll let you know with confidence and grace. I can say without a doubt that she is the sweetest, most adorable little girl I've ever known.

I also want to express my gratitude to some very special friends who have stood beside me, not only ensuring that I live by what I write and teach but who also bring out a greater version of myself. One of those friends is Phil Goldfine, an Academy Award–winning and Tony Award–winning producer. Phil is not only a student of the materials I teach, but he has also been my coteacher in many programs. I am proud to stand beside him and share the stage as we teach and mentor others. More importantly, I am proud to call him my friend.

I also want to thank my accountability and support partners, Arielle Ford, Brian Proctor, and Anders Hanson. We have been partners in success, committed to staying aligned with the goals taught in *The Moment of Alignment*. Their continued support and discipline in holding each other—and me—accountable over the years have been a gift, and I'm honored to have them in my life.

To my sister, Judy O'Beirn, my dear friends Jayne and Steve Lowell, Louise Tremblay, and countless others, your presence in my life is cherished more than words can say. I could fill an entire book with the names of those who have made a significant impact, but know that you are all in my heart.

I also want to take a moment to express my deep appreciation for someone who has been with me for many years and has truly been a cornerstone of my business: Roddy Telfer. His unwavering commitment to our prospects and clients is unparalleled. He has never said no when I've made requests, and despite the fast pace at which I move (sometimes overwhelming others), he remains steadfast, dedicated, and deeply caring. I am incredibly grateful to serve with him in my business. Roddy's kindness and generosity of spirit have made a lasting impact, and I am so fortunate to have him by my side. He is, without a doubt, invaluable.

I would also like to acknowledge G&D Media, my publisher, who believed in me and this book. Their unwavering support has been crucial in bringing *The Moment of Alignment* to life. I am deeply grateful for their belief in me and for their dedication to making this project a success.

I must also express my heartfelt thanks to my literary agent, Dan Strutzel. Dan has been an absolute joy to work with. He feels more like a partner than an agent, and I am truly grateful for his guidance and support throughout this journey.

Lastly, I want to express my deepest gratitude to my readers and clients. I believe I was put on this earth to serve people in positive, meaningful ways, and I am beyond grateful for the trust you place in me, in the information I share, and in the guidance I offer. It's always an honor to hear about your successes. As I often say, "My clients' success is my success," and I truly believe that to be the case. The work I do is enriched by your growth, and I look forward to all the success that is still to come.

There are many people in our lives for whom we can give thanks, and the practice of gratitude is both powerful and positive. I encourage everyone to embrace this practice. These are just a few of the many blessings for which I am forever grateful.

About the Author

Dr. Peggy McColl is a world-renowned expert in personal development, manifestation, and success conditioning. With over four decades of experience, she has inspired and empowered individuals across the globe to create lives of abundance, joy, and fulfillment. A *New York Times* best-selling author, Peggy has penned twenty-four transformational books that have been translated into multiple languages, touching the hearts and minds of readers in nearly 100 countries.

Driven by her passion for helping others achieve their highest potential, Peggy has built a thriving international business, guiding clients to align their thoughts, emotions, and actions with the results they desire. Her teachings blend metaphysical principles with practical, real-world strategies, making her one of the most sought-after mentors in the personal growth arena.

Peggy's unwavering belief in the power of the present moment has been the cornerstone of her success and the success of those she teaches. Through her programs, Masterminds, and private mentoring, she continues to show others how to harness the *moment of creation* to manifest extraordinary results.

In *The Moment of Alignment*, Peggy shares the profound insights and tools that have shaped her own life, guiding readers to step into their power and consciously create their ideal future.

When she isn't writing or mentoring, Peggy enjoys a joy-filled life with her husband, embracing each day with gratitude and purpose, and enjoying time with her precious grandchildren, James and Aria.

Go to http://PeggyMcColl.com for some valuable free gifts!

www.ingramcontent.com/pod-product-compliance
Lightning Source LLC
Chambersburg PA
CBHW072155070526
44585CB00015B/1152